Letters from Dr. Percy Magan

An Untold Story of Early Loma Linda

Albert Dittes

TEACH Services, Inc.
P U B L I S H I N G
www.TEACHServices.com • (800) 367-1844

All rights reserved. No part of this publication may be reproduced, distributed, or transmitted in any form or by any means, including photocopying, recording, or other electronic or mechanical methods, without the prior written permission of the publisher, except in the case of brief quotations embodied in critical reviews and certain other noncommercial uses permitted by copyright law. For permission requests, write to the publisher, TEACH Services, Inc., at the address below.

Copyright © 2022 Albert Dittes
Copyright © 2022 TEACH Services, Inc.
ISBN-13: 978-1-4796-1148-5 (Paperback)
ISBN-13: 978-1-4796-1149-2 (ePub)
Library of Congress Control Number: 2021935373

Published by

www.TEACHServices.com • (800) 367-1844

Dedication

I wish to dedicate this book to Frances Linda Dittes, a first cousin of my grandfather, Gotthold Dittes, and a distinguished professor of dietetics and nutrition at Madison College during its golden age. When I was growing up, she never ceased to marvel at the long range vision of E.A. Sutherland in encouraging Lida Scott to financially support the College of Medical Evangelists as well as Madison, its resulting impact on the Southern Union Conference of SDA, and felt strongly that this story should be told. Through her influence my father, Albert G. Dittes, attended Madison College, went on to graduate from the College of Medical Evangelists and worked as a physician for 53 years.

Table of Contents

Preface vii

Chapter 1: Setting the Stage— The Years 1910-1913 11

Chapter 2: The Real Work Begins—The Year 1916 15

Chapter 3: Another Source of Money Emerges—The Year 1917 23

Chapter 4: Progress Despite World War I Threats—The Year 1918 . . 37

Chapter 5: A New Era Opens—The Year 1919 53

Chapter 6: The Final Showdown—The Year 1921 69

Chapter 7: Loma Linda Marches On—Post-1921 Letters 85

Epilogue 103

Appendix 105

Endnotes 115

Preface

Right up until the end of her long and fruitful life, Ellen White went through the testing of her religious faith.

As a young woman, she had accepted the call of God to speak to her fellow believers through visions and dreams, and she had seen them result in the rise of a mighty religious movement with organized work all over the world. Though the passage of time had vindicated her counsels regarding churches, schools, hospitals, and publishing houses, one directive placed her in what she called "deep perplexity" in the summer of 1915.

She had seen in her visions and dreams that the church was to operate a fully accredited medical school in Southern California, centering it at Loma Linda. The idea of a small, unpopular religious movement like Seventh-day Adventism taking on such an undertaking was thought impossible by everyone, especially General Conference of SDA leaders fearful of embarrassing the church with debt. In his reminiscences, E. A. Sutherland, one of her devoted followers and founder of a college and sanitarium in Madison, Tennessee, based specifically on her counsels, recalled spending time with her at her Elmshaven home in Northern California and saying that it couldn't be done. He had just finished his M.D. degree. The American Medical Association would allow only one medical school per state, and that at a recognized university.

All Ellen White could tell him was that she had seen in a vision that Adventists were to have an accredited medical school educating physicians as competent as the world's best.

The Lord did not tell her where the money for this medical school would come from, however. And so she admitted to "deep perplexity" over Loma Linda to her son Willie White during her final days before dying in July, 1915, at the age of 87. At that time, Loma Linda offered a two-year course recognized by the medical profession. Upgrading it to a four-year, Grade A medical school would involve building a 100-bed teaching hospital in nearby Los Angeles at a cost of $61,000, or the equivalent of $1.22 million now.

In addition, the Lord did not reveal to her that the person who would make that possible had visited Elmshaven shortly before her death and afterward exchanged letters of condolence with Willie White. She was a wealthy woman from Montclair, New Jersey, named Lida Funk Scott, an heiress to the Funk & Wagnalls fortune. According to her correspondence, she gave $2,000 to the Loma Linda Sanitarium in the summer of 1915, possibly the donation that caused great comfort to Ellen White during this time of perplexity.[1]

Lida Scott herself did not then know what a critical role she would play in the rise of Loma Linda to full stature as a medical school. When Ellen White died in the summer of 1915, Lida Scott was recovering from personal tragedy, the death of her teenage daughter the year before. She had discovered the work of E. A. Sutherland in the southeastern United States with only a token Adventist presence and intended to financially support that.

But Sutherland had followed Ellen White's instruction to include a sanitarium as part of his school complex and encouraged his students to go out and do the same. These "units" of Madison needed physicians. He therefore supported upgrading the College of Medical Evangelists. His close friend and partner, Percy Tilson Magan, became dean of the medical school late in 1915. His job would be to raise money to develop a Los Angeles campus of the medical school to satisfy the demands of the American Medical Association for a teaching hospital in a population center owned and controlled by the school.

Sutherland told Mrs. Scott that if she wanted to help Madison, she would have to support the College of Medical Evangelists. The result was a remarkable correspondence between her and Percy Magan.

I uncovered this part of the Loma Linda heritage by finding letters between Percy T. Magan and Lida Scott at the Center for Adventist Research at Andrews University, Berrien Springs, Michigan. I thank the staff there for making these materials available to me. I also am grateful to the General Conference Office of Archives and Statistics for putting a complete set of the *Review and Herald* online, starting with the first issues of *Present Truth* magazine in 1849. Access to these magazines of that period also helped document the development of Loma Linda. Other important correspondence came from The Layman Foundation in Collegedale, Tennessee, and the Roger Goodge Collection at the Little Creek Nursing Home near Knoxville, Tennessee.

These letters reflect not only people putting their religious faith on the line and devoting themselves fully to accomplishing the mission of the Seventh-day Adventist Church but also the still-continuing struggle of the church to find the relationship of medical professionals to the evangelical proclamation of the gospel to every nation, kindred, tongue, and people.

    Albert Dittes
    Portland, Tennessee
    April 29, 2008

Setting the Stage

The Years 1910-1913

On the morning of May 29, 1913, the General Conference of Seventh-day Adventists, in session at Takoma Park, Maryland, devoted its 10:00 a.m. meeting to discussing a critical need of the Loma Linda Medical College in Southern California.[1]

"We know there is a difference of opinion regarding it, and we would like to have the one least interested in it, the one feeling most doubtful about it,--we would like to have your attention above all the rest, for we want to convert everybody that feels uncertain about it; at any rate, we want to come to a common understanding," said A. G. Daniells, president of the General Conference and chairman of the meeting. "Now just a word with reference to the object of the medical college. Its object is to furnish a medical school for Seventh-day Adventist young men and young women, in which they may receive thorough training as competent physicians, and from which they may be graduated to do the work we believe this denomination is called to do. That is the object. Now, if we still need physicians, if we ought to have our young people take the medical course and qualify for medical work, should we attempt to give them that education in our own institution, or should we not?"

According to the published minutes in the *Review and Herald*, many voices responded, "Sure!" "Amen!"

The assembly then heard two resolutions, one endorsing the work of making Loma Linda the center of physician training and the other recommending that Adventist young people go there for their medical education. Two other resolutions recommended that because the medical school needed more hospital and clinical facilities to carry on its work, the North American Division and the General Conference should advance the necessary funds there and encourage the church members to financially support it. Carrying out the latter would prove to be beyond the faith of most delegates.

The session approved the first two resolutions, and then came to the matter of raising money for the new hospital in Los Angeles. E. E. Andross said that the question of why to establish the medical school had come up at a 1910 biennial session of the Pacific Union. According to the record, I. H. Evans, treasurer of the General Conference; H. W. Cottrell, president of the Pacific Union at that time; and Andross, then president of the Southern California Conference, consulted Ellen White on the matter. To head off any accusation of using personal influence, the delegation did not visit her personally but asked for a written response if "she had any counsel from the Lord bearing directly upon the question under consideration," namely, "Are we to establish a thoroughly equipped medical school, the graduates from which shall be able to take State board examinations, and become registered, qualified physicians?"

She replied in the affirmative. "The light given me is, we must provide that which is essential to qualify our youth who desire to be physicians, so that they may intelligently fit themselves to be able to stand the examinations essential to prove their efficiency as physicians," Ellen White wrote. "They are to be prepared to stand the essential tests required by law, and to treat understandingly the cases of those who are diseased, so that the door will be closed for any sensible physician to fear that we are not giving in our school the instruction essential for the proper qualification of a physician. Continually the students who are graduated are to advance in knowledge; for practice makes perfect.

"The medical school at Loma Linda is to be of the highest order, because we have a living connection with the wisest of all physicians, from whom there is communicated knowledge of a superior order. And whatever subjects are required as essential in the schools conducted by those not of our faith, we are to supply, so that our youth need not go to these worldly schools."

Mrs. White then used a metaphor that several fund-raisers for the College of Medical Evangelists would quote in their *Review* articles.

"Thus we shall close a door that the enemy would be pleased to have left open; and our young men and young women, whom the Lord would have us guard religiously, will not need to connect with worldly medical schools conducted by unbelievers."

The source of the money to provide this advanced clinical training remained an issue, and some believers wondered whether the church should furnish the first two years of training at Loma Linda and then let the students finish in a prestigious, established medical school.

Ellen White said no, according to Elder Andross. "Some have advised that the students, after having taken some work at Loma Linda College, should complete their education in worldly colleges. But this is not in harmony with the Lord's plan. God is our wisdom, our sanctification, and our righteousness. Facilities should be provided at Loma Linda that the necessary instruction in medical lines may be given by the instructors who fear the Lord, and who are in harmony with his plans for the treatment of the sick. I have not a word to say in favor of the world's ideas of higher education in any school that we shall organize for the training of physicians. There is danger in their attaching themselves to worldly institutions, and working under the ministrations of worldly physicians. Satan is giving orders to those whom he has led to depart from the faith. I would now advise that none of our young people attach themselves to worldly medical institutions in hope of gaining better success or stronger influence as physicians."

That should have been orders enough to go ahead and develop the medical school into a four-year curriculum starting in 1910, but nothing had been done. Now it was 1913.

W. A. Ruble, president of the Loma Linda Medical College, told the delegates that even though the school had one of the best laboratories on the West Coast, its facilities covered only half a medical course. They would need a hospital and dispensary in Los Angeles to satisfactorily offer the second half, and money for this endeavor had not materialized. A lack of funds had halted construction. The American Medical Association wanted the medical college to build a hospital there with at least one hundred beds owned and controlled by the school.

"We needed twenty-five thousand dollars; we got eight thousand," he continued. "That has all been exhausted, and the workmen have been called off."

Dr. Ruble then explained the legitimacy of state standards.

"Medical men are compelled to undergo more rigid requirements than any other class of people among us. From the time they begin their study until they lie down in death, they are under strict medical laws, enacted by the governments under which they are operating. This is right. In taking into their hands the lives of men, medical men are given the greatest responsibility that is committed to any class of people; and so they should be under the most rigid laws, in order to carry out the instruction that we must carry out for the health of our people and others. . . . In establishing a medical school, we must submit to these laws, because we, as Seventh-day Adventists, claim to be the most law-abiding citizens in the world; and we are conscientious in this matter of meeting proper requirements."

Ruble added that his students received letters inviting them to finish their education at state medical schools, and that keeping them for medical missionary training at Loma Linda would be difficult without the adequate facilities.

"I cannot emphasize too strongly the necessity of acting promptly for the young people," he concluded. "There is no question but that we shall lose some of them unless something is done, and that quickly; because we must give them some assurance that we are to get the facilities that are necessary."

H. R. Salisbury and W. C. White argued persuasively that Adventist young people should receive their training at an Adventist-run school. The powerful I. H. Evans agreed. "I can scarcely think that a Seventh-day Adventist parent, under ordinary circumstances, would desire his child to be educated in any other medical institution than that of our people," he said. "I think the whole denomination ought to rally around this institution and make its work a splendid success, with a spirit of confidence, with a spirit of sympathy, with a spirit of cooperation."

W. T. Knox, treasurer of the General Conference, said that a special offering the previous March asking for $20,000 or more to meet this need had netted a disappointing $9,000. He estimated the school required an additional $17,500 to properly equip itself.

In other words, this money had come from church offering plates. The General Conference had agreed with the need but appropriated nothing.

"They must have the hospital; they must have clinical facilities," Knox continued. "They are already drawing to the close of the school year in which these facilities are needed from now on. How much better it will be for us to recognize the necessity, and provide for it at once, than to expose the school to the harm and the danger and the actual evil that result from being improperly equipped."

Dr. Ruble assured the assembly that Los Angeles would furnish the patient base to sustain a hospital in line with the teaching standards of the American Medical Association.

Somebody moved that the North American Division advance $17,000 to the medical school at once, but W. H. Thurston stated that the division treasury had no money, and W. A. McCutchen moved to refer the matter to the finance committees of the General Conference and North American Division.

The motion to refer carried.

The Real Work Begins

The Year 1916

On October 15, 1915, Augustus S. Downing, assistant commissioner for higher education of the New York State Department of Education, wrote to Dr. Newton Evans, president of the College of Medical Evangelists (CME) at Loma Linda, California, "that the College of Medical Evangelists Medical Department two-year course is not recognized by this Department and the Medical Department is not recognized to this department as leading to a degree which entitles graduates to our licensing examinations."[1]

In other words, no progress had been made in raising money for the hospital in the two years since the 1913 General Conference session. The issue would come up once again at the November Fall Council meeting in Loma Linda, California.

"I thank you for your letter of October 15, which was duly received," replied Dr. Evans on October 21. "If you will pardon my presumption in continuing the correspondence, I should like to ask you for some explanation of the statements of your letter.

"First, I do not exactly understand the meaning of the statement 'that the College of Medical Evangelists Medical Department two year course is not recognized by this department.' I cannot understand what is meant by this, as our Medical Department does not conduct any two year course.

"Secondly, in regard to the latter part of your statement that our 'Medical Department is not recognized to this department as leading to the degree which entitles graduates to our licensing examinations.'

"If you are able and willing to do so, I should very much appreciate the favor of a statement as to the reasons why our graduates should not be admitted to examination for license in the State of New York."[2] Dr. Downing was happy to oblige.

"I regret that my letter of October 15 was so obscure, incident to the necessity of my employing temporary, inefficient stenographic help," replied Dr. Downing on November 3.

Then he summed up the status of the medical school just prior to this important Fall Council meeting of the General Conference.

"The College of Medical Evangelists, Loma Linda, California, is accredited by this Department for two years of medicine. That is, the successful completion of the first three years of the five-year course entitles the applicant to two years' credit for admission on advanced standing to a 'registered' medical school. It follows that the successful completion of the first two years of the course can be accorded one year's credit only, and the successful completion of the first year course no credit.

"This accrediting was made when the institution was in process of organization and applied to the Regents for registration, June 22, 1912.

"The primary reasons why higher recognition could not be given lay in the inability of the institution to meet the Regents' requirements of 'at least six full time salaried instructors giving their entire time to medical work' and in the lack of suitable clinical facilities for the completion of 'a graded course of four full years of college work in medicine.'"[3]

The Loma Linda medical school definitely needed a teaching hospital in Los Angeles.

The Fall Council delegates hotly debated the issue and, in the end, voted to develop the four-year curriculum of the medical school on November 18, 1915. "In order to equip and properly complete the medical college at Loma Linda, California, it will be necessary to build in Los Angeles a hospital requiring an outlay of approximately $60,000," read an account of the meeting in the December 16, 1915, edition of the *Advent Review and Sabbath Herald*. "The constituency of the medical college voted to erect this building when the funds have been provided, so that there will be no further increase of indebtedness."[4]

In other words, the money would come from the field and not from the General Conference treasury.

One week after the vote, on November 25, 1915, the board of the College of Medical Evangelists elected 48- year-old Percy T. Magan of Madison, Tennessee, as dean of the new Los Angeles division. Magan had 20 years of experience in Adventist higher education behind him and had just graduated from medical school the year before. His job would be to develop a campus there meeting American Medical Association guidelines. Prominent women of the denomination, led by Mrs. S. N. (Hettie Hurd) Haskell, offered to help raise the needed money.

The *Review* printed their organizational structure. The Women's Committee on the Los Angeles Hospital consisted of a chairman and secretary. The North American Division treasurer handled the money, and "representative women" from each union and local conference promoted this urgent need in their particular fields. *The Review and Herald*--along with the local union conference papers--ublicized the campaign.[5]

The fund raising began immediately. An article by I. H. Evans, which appeared in the January 13, 1916, *Review and Herald*. pointed out that the brethren would be careful to build this $61,000 hospital as the funds arrived to avoid the embarrassment of debt. He introduced Hettie Haskell as the head of the fund-raising team and Dr. Percy T. Magan as the new dean of the Los Angeles campus of the medical school as well as set a deadline of September 15, 1916, for the $61,000 to be on hand.[6]

One of the first letters between Dr. Magan and a major donor who would become one of his chief benefactors surfaces about this time. Her name was Lida Funk Scott. Her father, Isaac Funk, co-founder of Funk & Wagnalls, had died in 1912 and left her a substantial fortune. She had become an Adventist in the late 1890s while she was a patient at the Battle Creek Sanitarium and took Bible studies from then Professor Magan. She had just become acquainted with the work of Magan and his close friend E. A. Sutherland at Madison, Tennessee, and made some donations to the Loma Linda campus of the medical school through the influence of Ellen White before she died.

A letter from Magan to Dr. Newton Evans about her dated February 28, 1916, said she had given $5,000 to Loma Linda but reflected some tension with the General Conference office.[7]

Lida Scott would soon give much more than that. She had apparently worked out an annuity agreement with the General Conference leaders due to thinking that a building program at the Los Angeles campus had been canceled. In the future, she would give directly to the College of Medical Evangelists.

Hettie Haskell wrote in the February 24 edition of the need for a thoroughly equipped medical school to train medical missionaries, citing Ellen White's statement of "godly physicians whose professional abilities are above those of the ordinary doctor" as the divinely ordained means to reach people living in the great cities. "They should seek to reach the higher classes," she continued quoting. "Medical missionaries who labor in evangelistic lines are doing a work of as high an order as are their ministerial fellow laborers. Where are these workers in our large cities? They are not to be found."

Mrs. Haskell also wrote that seven years earlier, Ellen White had told the General Conference in assembly, "Henceforth medical missionary work is to be carried forward with an earnestness with which it has never yet been carried. This work is the door through which the truth is to find entrance to the large cities." She added that it would be hard to train medical missionary workers in worldly schools.[8]

Percy Magan trumpeted the same theme in the next edition of the *Review*, also using the metaphor that it would "close a door that the enemy would be pleased to have left open" as citing the need for Adventist physicians to receive proper training from competent instructors who were also believers in the Advent message.[9]

In the March 16 *Review*, Dr. Magan noted that Southern California Adventist physicians had pledged $10,000 toward developing the Los Angeles campus. "Others made liberal promises, and steps were taken for a campaign to raise the money, so that, if possible, the dispensary may be completed by the fall opening of the school," he wrote.[10]

"The building of the hospital will go forward only as fast as the money is paid into the treasury," stated Mrs. Haskell in the April 13, 1916, *Review*. "No debts are to be incurred in erecting this building." She described the Loma Linda training school as being the youngest in the family of Seventh- day Adventist training institutions "but not by any means the least in importance. Like David (the youngest son of Jesse) it has a great work to accomplish for the up building of God's work in the earth."[11]

S. N. Haskell wrote that the three divisions of the Lord's great army are given as workers in educational lines, in ministerial and medical missionary lines. "In our North American Division we have five colleges and 23 academies, besides several seminaries, for the education and training of ministers and teachers," he continued. "While we have more than 30 advanced schools in America for the training of workers in the 'ministerial lines' and in the 'educational lines,' there are none of these schools that can give the necessary training that will fit one to do efficient work in 'medical missionary lines.'... We have spent hundreds of thousands of dollars in equipping colleges to train ministers and teachers. Why not equip *one* medical school to train workers in 'medical missionary lines?'"[12]

The April 20, 1916, *Review* reported pledges of $30,000 to $35,000 but only $258.34 in the treasury from individuals in the Atlantic, Northern, Pacific, and Southern Union Conferences.[13]

The record showed no pledge or contribution from the General Conference consisting of people knowing better than anybody about the legitimacy and urgency of this need.

I. H. Evans wrote a dramatic appeal asking for money to fund a church building in London, saying the General Conference had encouraged the Division there to raise $10,000. "Already the Northern Union Conference has contributed one thousand dollars, the Review and Herald has given five hundred, and individuals have given in smaller sums," he wrote. "So we have about seventeen hundred dollars already pledged to this splendid work.

"The need is certainly great, for in all Great Britain there is not a suitable place for our people to assemble," Elder Evans concluded. "They are especially in need of this meetinghouse for general meetings, and gatherings that must be held where the work is growing as it is in the British field. We therefore hope that the Division Conference will soon be able to pass this fund over in full to the General Conference for the purpose above named."[14]

On July 20 of that year, Evans appealed for "a large ingathering of funds for foreign missions and for the liquidation of the indebtedness on our institutions," adding that the church was far short of a full 20 cents per week per member. Of that money, 15 cents went to foreign missions and the rest to relieve institutional debts.[15]

The Women's Committee worked hard. The June 1, 1916, *Review* reported them "doing plain sewing" as well as making "iron-holders, boudoir caps, laundry bags, workbags, dresser scarfs, etc., for sale. Others can fruit, make jelly, preserves, salt-rising bread, cakes, marmalade, etc., which they sell. The Dorcas Society supplies quilts for $2.50. Still others sell milk, eggs, vegetables, etc."[16]

At the suggestion of Mrs. Haskell, Elders J. N. Loughborough, G. I. Butler, S. N. Haskell, H. W. Decker, and J. H. Rogers- -pioneer Adventist ministers over eighty years of age—allowed money from the sale of a group photo of them to go to the White Memorial Hospital, the first public mention of this name.[17]

One West Coast woman increased her commitment from $5,000 to $8,000, and a woman from the East gave $5,000 to build a dormitory. Their names did not appear in print

Mrs. Lotta Alsberge wrote that the women in the Northwestern California Conference had raised $409.20 in pledges and sales from the book *The Cross and Its Shadow* by S. N. Haskell.[18]

In the September 7 edition of the *Review*. I. H. Evans wrote that the North American Division had set Sabbath, October 14, as the date for a special offering to erect the Ellen G. White Memorial Hospital. "Sixty-one thousand dollars has been voted to this work on condition that we undertake to secure this by contributions," he said. "It is desired that on this occasion our brethren shall undertake to give at least one dollar per church member."[19]

But nothing would come from the conference treasury.

"Mother's views and plans regarding the work which was begun in 1905 by the purchase of the Loma Linda Sanitarium have always impressed me as being very broad and inclusive," wrote Willie White to answer an objection someone thought Ellen White would have to building a hospital in Los Angeles. "Often when expressing freely her views regarding the work in Southern California, she presented to our minds a united medical and evangelistic work which included Los Angeles, Redlands, Riverside, San Bernardino, and other places."

He added that in 1911 his mother had advised purchasing additional property around Loma Linda and also broadening the work there to include other cities in the area including Los Angeles. Then in March 1913, when building the hospital at Loma Linda was under consideration, she said that as much training as possible should be given at Loma Linda, but she saw no problem with the remainder being done in Los Angeles if necessary.

Just two months before her death, her son told her that a "good sister in the East" had offered to make a very liberal gift to the College of Medical Evangelists to establish a students' home and hospital in Los Angeles.

"Mother's lips quivered, and for a moment she shook with emotion. Then she said: 'I am glad you told me this. I have been in perplexity about Loma Linda, and this gives me courage and joy.'

"With such an experience as this, and knowing her anxiety in behalf of the Los Angeles department of the college work, I found no foundation for a doubt but that Mother would have been heartily glad if she could have known of the efforts that we were to make for the strengthening of the work, of which the Los Angeles hospital will be an important factor."[20]

And Percy Magan, anticipating that the $61,000 would be on hand, wrote Dr. Evans about the blueprints for the new White Memorial Hospital, having reviewed them carefully with Mrs. Scott and doing all he could to give her satisfaction.[21]

Dr. Newton Evans proudly shared the names of all the graduates to date of that young school and the places they served. Two of them had gone overseas—D. E. Davenport to China and Olive Smith to India. Hans and Dale Bonde lived in Calgary, Alberta, Canada. H. C. Nelson was at the Portland Sanitarium in Portland, Oregon. Leslie Butka worked at a sanitarium in New York. Most of them lived in California: O. S. Parrett, Fred and Lavina Herzer, L. M. White, J. J. Weir, A. R. Dickson, A. N. Donaldson, O. Santee- Donaldson, Zenobia Nightengale, C. W. Harrison, A. W. Semmens, W. Richli, John Warren, Mary Zener, Leslie Trott, Lawrence Butka, Arabelle Feldkamp, Josie Shryock, R. M. Smith, Geoffrey Williams, and Iner Ritchie.

"With the addition of the medical evangelistic courses and the extending and perfecting of the work in the various departments of the regular medical school, it has become necessary to add a number of physicians and assistants to our staff of workers here in the college and sanitarium, opening the way for many of our own graduates to remain here," wrote Dr. Evans. "This accounts for the apparently large proportion in Loma Linda, but all who have been graduated are as ready to respond to calls for the needy fields near or far, as were those who have gone. Only two out of the 28 are in private practice, and these two stand ready to enter our work when the way opens."[22]

The *Review* did not print the amount of money that was received on October 14, but it fell short of the needed $61,000 for the hospital.

"Like most new enterprises, the women's committee work has not sailed in unruffled seas," wrote Mrs. Haskell in the November 2 *Review*. "The success of the enterprise depended upon the cooperation of our brethren throughout the field. Some of the Union Conferences appointed secretaries early in the year; but for various reasons the work was late in getting started in other Unions, and it was not until the latter part of the summer that the work began to be fostered in the field at large."

She commended Elder E. E. Andross, president of the Pacific Union, for his help in raising $6,200 plus some other donations by wealthy individuals in that part of the Division. The Western Canadian Union women raised $1,344 in cash and pledges. She reported printing 37,000 copies of the leaflet "Preparedness" and 10,000 copies of the tract "The Need of The Ellen G. White Memorial Hospital." The committee also sent out more than 1,000 letters in the interest of the hospital fund and labored in nine different conferences.

"We regret very much that the present organization could not have been formed at the beginning of the year, so that the complete work for which the committee was appointed might have been accomplished," she concluded. "We wish to thank the brethren for the privilege of having some part in helping to equip our medical school which we earnestly pray may be used of God to educate an army of medical missionaries for the closing of the work."[23]

The Fall Council of the North American Division expressed "thanks and deep appreciation" to the Women's Committee for its work in raising funds for the proposed Los Angeles hospital, and added "that, as we hope to realize from the offering taken October 14 sufficient funds for the erection of the hospital, making the work of the auxiliary committee no longer necessary, it be understood that the Women's Auxiliary Committee is therefore discontinued."[24]

Interestingly, a resolution approved by this same council reflected their tardiness in funding money for the White Memorial Hospital. They gave serious attention to bringing the Adventist message before people in the large cities but found no role for physicians in this great undertaking.

The council recommended this strategy for city evangelism:

- Every member win at least one soul to Christ during the coming year.
- Every paid conference worker undertake a stronger and more active soul-winning campaign.
- All departments and administrative boards assist in the soul-winning efforts as best they can.
- Support strong public efforts to reach the unwarned cities.
- Make greater use of the public press in proclaiming the truth.
- Form strong evangelical teams to work the larger population centers.
- Train nurses to become efficient Bible workers in the cities.
- Train competent Bible workers to follow up all interests.

"Owing to the rapid fulfillment of prophecy pointing unmistakably to the nearness of the end," read the preamble, "it behooves this people, and especially the workers representing this movement, to use all diligence in winning souls to Christ, and to proclaim the third angel's message in all its fullness, that many may be prepared against that day of wrath."[25]

Another Source of Money Emerges

The Year 1917

While a lack of funds prevented construction of the White Memorial Hospital at the end of 1916, enough money was on hand to build a dispensary on the Boyle Heights property surrounded by Boyle Avenue and New Jersey, Bailey, and Michigan Streets. An open air service was held on December 1 to inaugurate its beginning. "The work of erecting this first building, the dispensary, is going forward rapidly, and it is planned, as soon as this building nears completion, to begin at once the erection of the students' dormitories, the money for which is already in hand," wrote Dr. Newton Evans in the *Review and Herald*.

At the service, Elder W. F. Martin, president of the Southeastern California Conference, compared the complex to Solomon's Temple in that every great movement among God's people had centralized around a building. Dr. A. W. Truman pointed out the importance of building life-saving stations in a time of so much death and destruction during the World War I the United States had not yet entered. He also read several Spirit of Prophecy statements saying Adventist young people should receive a complete medical education in a Seventh-day Adventist setting. Prominent woman physician Dr. Abbie Winegar-Simpson agreed. Dr. George Thomason, a longtime medical missionary, referred to that plot of ground as "a center from which God's messengers will go to earth's remotest bounds, bearing the gospel of life and salvation."

Other speakers were Elder J. O. Corliss, Dr. G. K. Abbott, and Dr. D. D. Comstock.

"The funds are coming in in a most encouraging way, and are much in excess now of the amount required for the buildings which are to be erected at once," Dr. Evans concluded. "However, the amount which was to be raised for the hospital--$61,000, in all—has not yet been reached, and it is earnestly hoped that pledges and donations will come in steadily, in order that the needed hospital facilities may be secured without delay."[1]

Just a few months later, on April 6, 1917, the United States entered World War I on the Allied side and forced the hospital need onto a back burner, at least temporarily. All young men became subject to the armed forces draft, and it would be hard to persuade the U.S. Army to exempt the Loma Linda students if they attended a C-rated medical school. This situation put extreme pressure on Dr. Magan to use his contacts in high places to elevate the schools' rating to Grade B. The SDA Church also wanted non-combatancy status for its young men, a situation causing conflict with some government officials. He proposed that the medical school set up a base hospital in France to help the war effort, something that generated much talk but never happened. To enable the church to help the war effort and be faithful to its ideals of not taking life, he arranged a meeting of denominational leaders with U.S. Food Commissioner Herbert Hoover to work out a program of food conservation.[2]

Dr. Magan's correspondence with Lida Scott, a wealthy woman recovering from personal tragedy, reflected his high and low points during that critical year for the medical school when political pressures threatened to bring the entire operation to a halt. It also showed him to be a master at fund raising.

"I cannot tell you how pleased I was today to receive your long and very interesting letter of February 8th," he wrote to her (February 15, 1917) at her Montclair, New Jersey, home. "I had become quite worried about you, but am so thankful to know that you are much better and still keeping up your treatments and rest hours. This is splendid."[3]

He had a great deal to tell about that year.

"Sunday I went down to Anaheim to the camp meeting, and had a long visit with Elder Daniells," he wrote in summing up his tangled relationship with the General Conference that year in 1917. "He feels the present situation amongst our brethren at Washington very, very keenly. He feels there is no vision amongst them, no big desire to do great things for God and His cause, and a wretched, visionless policy, which will never get us anywhere."[4]

An emergency council to handle the pressures of World War I met at Loma Linda on July 3 and 4, 1917.

"The facts are, we have had a tremendous time at the meeting at Loma Linda," he wrote to Mrs. Scott on July 9. "If ever the Lord led me into anything which worked out showing there were mighty providences back of it, it has been this matter of the base hospital and the Loma Linda summer school and conference. Daniells, Knox, G. E. Thompson, all the leading physicians and business managers of sanitariums on the Pacific Coast, and the heads of the Pacific Press were present, besides a large concourse of brethren and sisters. The meeting was the most harmonious, the most spiritual, and the most full of courage I have attended in many a long day.

"Dr. Sutherland was called upon to present the food question, and it was enthusiastically voted that we recommend to the North American Division Conference that the denomination establish a food commissioner, and that we organize the denomination for food conservation work the country over. We have already organized here on the Pacific Coast, and have begun operations on a big scale.

"I was asked to present the matter of the base hospital, and it was unanimously voted that we organize that. Elder Daniells and Dr. Thomason made peace. Sutherland and I have been advised to go to Washington immediately to confer with the government officials on these matters. I leave here Friday afternoon, reaching Nashville Monday evening. Hope to get away Tuesday evening, and it may be, as afore stated, that Wednesday evening we can drive out to your place and see you for a little bit."[5]

He had grave business in Washington, D.C. The war had adversely affected the relationship of the church and the government.

He shared with her that the Governor Thomas Clarke Rye of Tennessee tried to make things difficult for Seventh-day Adventists: "Now I will endeavor to tell you a little in regard to my visit to Washington. I left here the 13th of July and went to Nashville. There Dr. Sutherland and I met, and found rather a complicated state of affairs in regard to our brethren and service in the army. The governor of the state took the ground that if we did anything for the government, such as nursing the sick; we were in so doing waiving our right to the exemption, which the law gives in bearing arms. The governor was quite stirred up about the matter and seemed determined to force us to bear arms."

Magan knew what to do.

"In this emergency our old friend, Dr. E. M. Sanders, came to our rescue. He is a member of the Governor's staff, and I suppose the best friend we have in the city of Nashville. He became quite angry with the Governor, and told him he intended to go to Washington himself and look into the matter, so when Sutherland and I were ready to go, Dr. Sanders came along with us."

He then shared a little insight on how going to medical school while a college professor in Madison, Tennessee, benefited him politically as well as professionally.

"I don't know whether I have ever told you how it was that Dr. Sanders became interested in us in the first place. It was when Dr. Sutherland and I were attending the Medical College of the University of Tennessee. I passed 100 on the mid-term examination in Anatomy, which subject he taught. He only gave me 91, making a statement to the class that he withheld the higher grade because I had not attended on Sabbath. A number of the men in the class became angry with him for this, and they had a pretty hard set-to over it. When I heard about it I went to see him, and told him that what he had done was perfectly all right with me, that I was very thankful to get through at all, and had no criticism to make on the way he had done. He seemed very much touched, and that was the beginning of a friendship, which has lasted until the present time."

Abiding with his teacher's decision paid off.

"When we arrived in Washington we went to see the Representative in Congress from our district in Tennessee, Mr. Joseph Byrns. He was exceedingly kind to us, and took the ground that Governor Rye did not know what he was talking about, but that in order to make sure of the whole matter he would see that we had an interview with General Crowder, who is Provost-Marshall General of the army. He also advised us, if possible, to see the Attorney General of the United States.

"We went to see the Attorney General. While waiting in the outer office one of the assistant attorneys attached to his staff whom we knew, came and told us we would never get to see him; that thousands of people came there to see him and were not admitted, and that he never talked to anyone on matters of business beside the President of the United States and his cabinet. Just as this attorney was talking to us, the chief clerk came out and said, 'Attorney-General Gregory will see the gentlemen from Tennessee at 4:30 this afternoon,' and at 4:30 we saw him and spent over an hour with him, got all the information we wanted, and a complete vindication of our rights.

"The way in which we came to get in to see him, to me, [is] one of those providences which God arranges from a long way back. When General Gregory was a very poor and very green boy, at the close of the Civil War, he came from the State of Mississippi to Clarksville, Tennessee. In that little burg there was at that time a law school of quite a little renown in the South. He had just money enough to pay his tuition, but not one cent for board and room. Wandering around the town wondering what he could do, someone told him of a very hospitable and godly woman who might possibly give him his board and room—a Mrs. Hattie Kendrick. Boy like, he took a chance, and went to see her, and told her his story and how anxious he was to obtain an education in the law. She listened to him graciously, and after hearing his tale said, 'Well, my boy, I will give you your board and room as long as you are in the law school and provided you will give me your promise always to be early in the evening, never to smoke or drink or use bad language and every Sunday to accompany me and my daughters to church.' Gregory looked up and said, 'Miss Hattie, I will most certainly do all that you ask, and be deeply grateful; and, at the same time, I want to tell you that you are the most beautiful woman I have ever laid eyes on.' To which this gracious Southern dame replied, 'If you ever make that remark again, I will put you out of the house and never let you come back in again.' Mrs. Hattie Kendrick was, and though she is now past 70 years of age, still is a most beautiful woman, and one of the most noble souls I have ever known. Attorney-General Gregory raves over her beauty to this day. Whenever he is in the South he goes to see her, and feels that his great success in life has been largely due to the kindness which she showed him in the early days.

"But Mrs. Hattie Kendrick is the mother of Dr. Sanders' wife, and that is where we become connected up with the story. When Mrs. Sarah Sanders, E. M. Sanders' wife, sent her mother a telegram telling her that her husband and Dr. Sutherland and Dr. Magan wanted to see the Attorney-General, Mrs. Hattie Kendrick immediately sent him a telegram asking him if he would not, for the sake of his old friend and benefactress, see her friends from Tennessee. This is how we came to see the Attorney General."[6]

His visits with Dr. Franklin H. Martin of Chicago and a member of President Wilson's Advisory Commission of the National Defense resulted in the base hospital unit idea to help with the war effort and also brought up another critical issue.

"I also had two or three long visits with Dr. Franklin Martin, concerning whom you have heard me speak before," he wrote. "He again expressed himself as deeply desirous that we should get the hospital unit underway as soon as possible."[7]

After the College of Medical Evangelists obtained a B rating, the Surgeon General allowed its students to return to school. "The government has exempted our second, third, and fourth year medical students, so Wellesley [one of his three sons] is safe. We do not know yet how it is going to be about the first year."[8]

Magan didn't have a friend with access to Herbert Hoover, but he managed to set up a fruitful meeting with him.

"We also had an excellent visit with Mr. Hoover. From him we learned that practically all the other denominations in the land were already organized and taking hold of the food work to the best of their ability. He was very glad to know that we were interested in the matter too. He told us that he would meet our leading men any time we set the hour. We left, promising to make proper arrangements with our people and to notify him later.

"The next day we had an interview with General Crowder, in which he promised that our youth should be exempt from bearing arms provided that as a denomination we could show to his credit that we were entitled to the exemption. He was very gracious to us, and seemed interested in us."

Setting up this meeting with Commissioner Hoover brought out the differences with the General Conference brethren once again, perhaps showing why they stalled in appropriating money for the needed hospital.

"Then we went out to Takoma Park," he wrote to Mrs. Scott. "Elder Daniells had not yet arrived. Dr. Sutherland saw Elder I. H. Evans and had a brief talk with him. I had a bad foot and did not accompany Dr. Sutherland on this visit. Elder Evans was very bold, and seemed absolutely without interest in anything that we were doing or trying to do, so Sutherland did not waste much time with him. Dr. Sanders had desired to meet our leading men, so as Daniells was not there, and Evans was as cold as the iceberg that sank the Titanic, Sutherland promptly decided not to bring Sanders out to Takoma Park as he did not think the reception would be a very interesting one.

"Finally Daniells came. We told him all that we had done, and he was very much pleased, and told us to go ahead and arrange for the meeting with Hoover and he would see Elder Evans. We did this, arranging for 10 o'clock of the following Tuesday morning. Early Monday we notified Elder Daniells to this effect, and he told us it was all right and that he would see Elder Evans.

"That afternoon a meeting of all the leading brethren in Takoma Park was held, at which we were present. Elder Daniells related the story of the good meeting we had had at Loma Linda, and spoke very highly in regard to our physicians and the medical work that was being done. He told the different steps that had led up to the idea of forming the base hospital, and also in regard to the food matter, and how Sutherland had been appointed Food Commissioner of the State of Tennessee.

"It was easy to see while he was talking that the crowd was not pleased. He wound up by telling them that an appointment had been made with Hoover the next morning at 10 o'clock; and then the storm bell rang, and the curtain arose on quite a troubled scene. I. H. Evans said that he did not care to meet Mr. Hoover; that he did not believe in chasing after noted men; that if he wanted to live health reform he could live it without Hoover's help. Spicer came next with a speech, stating that he thought we ought not to go and see Hoover at all, at least not until after all the brethren had come in from around the country and decided whether they wanted to see him. Upon this someone else piped up and said it was a shame the appointment had been made, but now that it was made they would not know what to do, for if they told Hoover they would not meet him the next day, and then counseled over the matter and decided they would not meet him at all, they would be in a bad fix with the Government, whereas if they should go according to our appointment, their pride would be woefully hurt.

"I was about to make a speech when Sutherland kicked me two or three times, and told me to shut up, adding, 'They've got to go, Magan, they've got to go. Watch them wriggle, but see them come.' So I kept my mouth shut, and we waited and listened to the angry speeches that came thick and fast.

"Evans said that we had not consulted him about the matter, and he did not know what business it was of ours anyway, but he supposed he would have to go; so finally they voted to go.

"The next morning Sutherland and I had to go downtown early and see Dr. Franklin Martin. I had wind of it that Evans and his friends were stating that they had a letter from the Red Cross saying that if we did organize a hospital for France we would have to pay all salaries all the time the organization was over there, as the government would not do it. I knew this was wrong, so I asked Martin to write me a letter to that effect, which he did, letting me dictate just what I wanted, and he signing it.

"Then we went over to Hoover's office. Mr. Cullen, who has charge of the work among the churches, was there, and we told him that the brethren would all be there by 10 o'clock. Cullen was very pleased. We told him we had had quite a hard time with them, and laughed about it together. Then he showed me the big committee room where we were to meet, and said, 'Now, I want you to sit beside me and tell me whom to call on for speeches amongst your people.'

"Soon the brethren trooped in, 37 in all, and took their places all around the room. Then in came Mr. Hoover and Dr. Ray Lyman Wilbur, president of Leland Stanford University, and chief man under Hoover in the Food Administration matter. Both of these men made excellent speeches. As soon as I copy off the notes I made from them I will send you copies of the same, as I am sure you will enjoy them. You know Hoover is a Quaker, and is really an exceedingly interesting personage.

"When these speeches were over, Hoover and Wilbur went out, and Cullen asked me whom he should call on to offer prayer. I naively told him to call upon Elder I. H. Evans, which he promptly did, and Evans had to call upon the Lord to bless the meeting, which he had been cursing for the last 24 hours. Then Cullen made an excellent talk, telling us of his knowledge of our people, of his interest in us, and how Hoover had told him that he, Hoover, knew that we were non-combatants and that we ought to be especially interested in the food business. Cullen told how he would like us to appoint a food commissioner of our own as a denomination, and have the chairman of it spend a while with him in his office in Washington getting on to the way they were doing things.

"Then I told Cullen to call on Evans for a speech, which he did, and once again Baalaam had to bless that which he had cursed. Next I told Cullen to call on Elder Daniells, who made an excellent talk, full of feeling and pathos. Mr. Hoover in his speech had made the point to us that we were not helping to kill Germans, but to feed poor old men and women and little children. He said that there was no question but that the armies would be fed, and that the service we effected would be a blessing to these poor people."

Back at church headquarters, the fur continued to fly.

"That afternoon the first meeting of the council of the brethren took place at Takoma Park. Elder Evans gave an excellent talk, telling about the troubles and trials in which our people were and advocating that we do all in our power to work with the government in every way possible. He then called on me to tell what Sutherland and I had done in meeting government officials in Washington. This I did, but I saw very clearly as I went along that it was not setting very well with the Washington magnates.

"When I finished Elder F. M. Wilcox talked, telling in a gentle and quiet manner how he was afraid we would get entangled with the government;

and after that Spicer made a similar talk; and then W. W. Prescott turned loose, and declared that we must not do anything to work with the government in any way whatsoever; that he was opposed to our taking hold of the food conservation; opposed to a base hospital; he accused us of forcing ourselves on the government; declared that to do anything would be to make an image to the beast, and unite church and state. He read from a letter I had written someone in which I stated that Major Kirby-Smith, of the Red Cross, had told me that the government did not want any more base hospitals, and he accused me of trying to give them something they didn't want. In the same paragraph in that letter I had written how Dr. Franklin Martin, the chairman of the Medical Section of the Council on National Defense, had told me that they did want a base hospital from us; but Prescott did not read that part.

"The next morning I. H. Evans opened up with a very violent speech. He accused Daniells, Thompson, Knox and myself of pretty nearly every crime in the Decalogue. He declared to do anything to assist the government in this crisis was to violate every principle we as a denomination had ever held in regard to the separation of church and state. He charged us with having bad motives, and of courting the favor of noted men. He, by a wonderful process of asinine mathematics, figured out that we would have to furnish 200 men and women a month to run the hospital, and then he informed us that the government would not pay the salaries of the personnel of the hospital. Then he told us that Sister White had said in the days of the Civil War, that the generals of the armies were under the control of the devil, and that if we entered into this hospital proposition we would be under the control of generals, and consequently under the control of the devil. Then he stated that I had told him that we could not preach the message in the hospital unless we did it on the sly. Then he added, 'Who wants to send their daughter to that immoral hell to act as a nurse, when the only result would be that she would lose her virtue?' Then he banged his book shut, and said, 'Now we are done with this thing, and we won't consider it any more.'

"Immediately Flaiz took the floor, and gave a discourse on corsets, high heels, and low-necked frocks. Just exactly what this performance had to say to food conservation and base hospitals I don't know, but his great burden seemed to be for women's clothes. For an hour and a half he talked that stuff.

"When he got through Will White demanded the floor, and after a recess had been taken, obtained it. He began by stating that at first when he heard of the base hospital proposition he had been opposed to it, but that all the arguments he had heard against it at this meeting had converted him to it, and that he sincerely hoped that it would go through; but that in view of the fact that a great many charges had been made, thought that either Elder Daniells or I ought to make an apology or a confession.

"Daniells nodded me to go on, so I began my confession of faith.

"I started in by telling them that the whole performance reminded me of a time when Elder S. N. Haskell had made a contract with the British Government in South Africa by which they were to give the Seventh-day Adventist church 6,000 acres of land on condition that we would start a mission on it to civilize and Christianize the natives. How that at the General Conference of that year in Battle Creek A.T. Jones, Prescott, and others had stormed and raved, and said he was violating every sacred principle of church and state, and had gotten the conference to vote that we should not accept the land; and how afterwards a testimony had come from Sister White saying that their views on church and state were clouded and needed a vision, and that God always had men in high places in governments to befriend his people and help them in their work. I told Evans and Prescott that in my judgment they were doing precisely the same thing that had been done there.

"Then I took up the accusation that I had been running after noted men, and told the story of how we had come to know Claxton, Gregory and Martin. I showed how that in each case it had been a providence of God that had thrown us in the way of these men, and that the time might come when men who were not shouting so loudly against acquaintances with prominent men might be mighty thankful to have a few friends among them in high circles. I showed how the Lord had done this all through the days of the Bible; how He had raised up Cyrus, Nebuchadnezzar and other men to befriend the people of God in a time of need."[9]

Lida Scott seemed to feel a bit guilty about a busy man writing her so much, but Dr. Magan had no problem with fully informing her.

"Do not feel that it was any task for me to send you such a long letter about affairs in Washington at the time of our meeting there," Magan wrote to Mrs. Scott on September 21, 1917. "I feel that you have done so much to help real true medical missionary work along that we owe you a great deal more than any little remembrance like this. It certainly was a great experience. I am telling our students in our Bible class now for a few days the bright parts of the story, and we are having great times together.

"I will always feel that the Lord wonderfully worked for us with the government officials in Washington. Elder Daniells feels the same way. I am sure you are right when you say that God is not discouraged with us. He has planned things years in advance in raising up friends for us in this crisis, and if we will be true to Him and His principles he will demonstrate this more and more."[10]

His other letters to Mrs. Scott illustrated that the complicated relationships with church and government officials in Washington were not the only things on his mind.

"We are getting our self-government plan started here with the medical and medical evangelistic students, and it is going well. Of course, a great deal of educational work will have to be done, and it will take time, but it is working in a manner for which I feel very thankful."[11]

He provided details of the dispensary design. "I am so glad you like the plan that our Dispensary is being built on. I have been studying very earnestly the Testimonies' on the matter of our buildings, and have made a number of interesting notes and extracts. Probably I will have these mimeographed a little later, and if you would like a copy I will be glad to send it to you.

"There has been quite an influence at work here to have a large fireproof building put up for the main hospital, but I think I have succeeded absolutely in killing this. There is a statement in the Spirit of Prophecy that no building that we can erect is fireproof, and that putting up structures of this kind speaks against our faith that the Lord is coming soon.

"Again, I am sure that building our plant on the cottage plan will give it a much more 'homey' appearance than to have one large building, which often fills the patient with horror on account of its general hospital appearance."[12]

He wanted more than money. "While I think of it, I am getting a little money in a quiet way for a nucleus for a little library for our nurses and medical students in Los Angeles. At present we do not have as much as one book down there. I wonder if it will be possible for you, when the time comes, to secure us a low price on one of the big Dictionaries which the Funk and Wagnalls Company publishes—the Standard I believe it is. I do not want you to do this if it will be embarrassing for you in any way, but if it can be done I would appreciate being able to save whatever will be saved by the special price you might secure for us. I expect you will think I am a beggar, but as I tell some of them 'that's my business.'"[13]

He also made it his business to attract students. "You will be glad to know that I have an invitation to visit almost all of our denominational colleges and academies before school closes this spring, and talk with them in regard to our medical missionary work. This is a great opportunity, and I am praying that the Lord will give me wisdom to have so much of his spirit in connection with this work that I will be able to interest a large number of young people in it, so I expect I will get down your way before very many months have gone by."[14]

The correspondence showed a deepening financial involvement by Mrs. Scott in the work at Loma Linda as well as helping Magan's son Shaen pay his medical school tuition.[15]

Shaen was one of three sons of Percy T. Magan. He married Ida May Bauer June 14, 1892. They had two sons: Wellesley Percy, born August 7, 1893, and Shaen Saurin, born September 24, 1896. His first wife died on May 19, 1904. After moving to Madison, Magan married Dr. Lillian Eshleman on August 23, 1905. They had one son, Val O'Connor, born January 19, 1912.

Lida Scott initially approved naming a cottage on the new White Memorial Hospital campus in honor of her late daughter Helen, who had died in the summer of 1914, but her husband decided he didn't want the name associated with Ellen White. (Dr. John Harvey Kellogg had told him that Ellen White was a plagiarist.) Magan changed the name to Montclair Cottage.

"I hope to have a photograph of your cottage for you very soon," he wrote. "It is really a beautiful building, and I am only sad that we cannot use your daughter's name on it. We expect now in a few days to start erecting the first unit of the hospital proper. The Lord is certainly wonderfully blessing us in this matter."[16]

Locally, things were looking up.

"You will be interested to know that one of the leading physicians of the city was here day before yesterday and went through your cottage, and was so pleased with it. He talked with me at least an hour about our whole dormitory system, about our plan for boarding our students, etc."[17]

"We are home again," she wrote to him on July 6, 1917. "I wish you could have seen how beautiful our grounds look this year with nearly 150 rosebushes in bloom, and a score of climbing roses of different varieties. Mr. Scott's vegetable garden is blossoming, not like the rose, but only as potatoes, radishes, legumes, etc., can blossom. We planted about a pint of peas and have already picked over a bushel in the pods; everything else seems to be thriving proportionately. Mr. Scott is delighted with his first attempt.

"I am doing fine these days. I am having no treatments, and am sleeping more naturally at night than I have done since last September, but I find I cannot attempt taking any responsibility. Miss Hibben carries the responsibilities of home for me most admirably, and insists she will not leave me until I am able to resume them. It is lovely of her to do this, but I am not sure that I am doing right to permit her to do so."[18]

She did feel good enough to sense the old tensions with the General Conference officers.

"Why do you suppose those people at Washington wanted to know whether or not I was at Madison?" she wrote to him. "Brother Enoch, who has been very urgent for more than a year that I should increase my donation to Washington College, went to Madison himself about that time. It was a curious coincidence though I do not suppose the two incidents were at all related. Our leading men are beginning to wonder what there is at Madison to so powerfully hold the people's interest, and I suppose they think they must go there to find out. Well, they will find out, if they are in earnest and will stay long enough.

"I shall look forward to your letter telling me about your experiences with the brethren at Washington and also the summer school at Los Angeles with deep interest. It seems so strange that our Washington brethren are so fearful of the Mark of the Beast in this matter while all the time they are getting the Mark of the Beast in the system of education they are adopting. Dr. Sutherland just dropped us enough of a hint for us to know they were afraid they would get the Mark of the Beast if they established a base hospital. Aside from this he gave us no information whatever as we expected you in a few days, and, as I had not had a very good sleep the night before, I did not put to him any questions on this subject. I am sorry now I didn't. I was very glad to have Dr. Sutherland meet Mr. Scott, and we were glad to get that glimpse of him ourselves.

"My, I do hope the time will soon come when the best of our people will rise up and refuse to be led by men who have no vision, and who do not stand true to educational and medical reforms. I thank God that you and Dr. Sutherland have the *courage* of your convictions. ... l am glad to hear that Elder Daniells is standing true."[19]

The year 1917 closed dramatically at the College of Medical Evangelists with the unfolding of a remarkable Adventist story of sacrifice. Percy Magan came up with the money to build the needed hospital.

The November 29, 1917, *Advent Review and Sabbath Herald* ran a startling announcement in its minutes of the Fall Council for that year. The General Conference would advance up to $20,000 to enable the College of Medical Evangelists to "proceed immediately with the erection of the two additional units to the hospital in Los Angeles in order that these buildings may be ready for use by the opening of the next college year."

The denomination had finally come through.

"Representatives of the Loma Linda College of Medical Evangelists met with the council for a few days," according to the Review account of the meeting. "It seemed imperative, for various reasons, that additional units should be provided for the hospital without further delay."[20]

To meet this desperate financial need, with everything now depending on building this hospital in Los Angeles to satisfy the American Medical Association requirements, Magan once more turned to his Tennessee friends. His college roommate, Ed Sutherland, had the gift of attracting big donors. One of them, Josephine Gotzian, with the encouragement of Dr. Sutherland, had given the first $10,000 of monies enabling Magan to buy the Boyle Heights property for the Los Angeles campus of the medical school.

Now, with time running out for starting the needed hospital, Magan put a 30-year friendship on the line and asked Sutherland if he would allow $30,000 that Lida Scott had promised Madison College to go to the College of Medical Evangelists instead. If she would do that, the General Conference would match it with another $30,000. (Magan had to come up with the first half of the required amount.)

"That was a hard request for me to agree to," Sutherland wrote years later. "I recognized that it was only natural for Dr. Magan to seek help from his old Madison friends, and past experience had given us so much confidence in the integrity of each other that we were bound to cooperate when one of us needed help.

"I was convinced that his request was reasonable, and we both went to Mrs. Scott and told her of the great need of help for the College of Medical Evangelists," Sutherland continued. "She hesitated at first but soon saw that the self-supporting work in the South could not prosper without doctors and that there was no way of securing them except from the College of Medical Evangelists and so gave him $30,000."[21]

Financially struggling, self-supporting Madison College continued to do without for the time being while the Ellen G. White Memorial Hospital took shape.

Progress Despite World War I Threats

The Year 1918

"Your letter of December 24th giving so many interesting details, I assure you was much enjoyed," wrote Lida Scott to Dr. Magan (January 25, 1918) from her comfortable home in Montclair, New Jersey, to start the new year. "I appreciate the trouble you take in these busy and anxious days. Surely the days spoken of by Sister White, when every soul will have to meet its test alone, are hastening on apace. It is encouraging to read your personal experiences as to how the Lord takes care of the consequences when you take Him at His word, and how He guards His children from the devices of Satan."

Though hospital construction was finally under way, the future of the medical school was still in doubt.

"Mr. Scott had a conversation with Dr. Kellogg in New York," she continued, "having had him out to lunch, in which Dr. Kellogg said the standard of Loma Linda would never be raised, and that the Medical Association would never stand for a denominational medical college; so when Mr. Scott brought the information home I was glad I could say quietly, 'It has already been raised.' Mr. Scott was astonished, and I think since then he has realized that Dr. Kellogg's word is not necessarily final. From a remark he made the other night I can see that he thinks Dr. Kellogg is prejudiced against our people."

Dr. John Harvey Kellogg had been the first Seventh-day Adventist physician to show what could be done with medical missionary work by developing the Battle Creek Sanitarium in Michigan into a world-famous institution. He had lost a political battle with A.G. Daniells eleven years before and been dismissed from church membership. Some graduates of his medical school, now closed, became early faculty members of the College of Medical Evangelists.

Mrs. Scott clearly had unwavering faith in the mission of Loma Linda.

"Surely the Lord will bless such men as Dr. Colwell, the Surgeon General at Washington, Dr. Martin, General Crowder, and others, for the kindly interest they have shown in our school and in returning our boys from the camps. How I should have enjoyed being at the celebration on New Year's Day, but I am keeping pretty quiet these days, and could not think of taking a trip like that at present with transportation so poor. I do not even expect to attend the General Conference."

New Year's Day of 1918 had been a big day for the medical school to give thanks for the 1917 victories. The denomination was also coming into its own. The General Conference of Seventh-day Adventists would meet in San Francisco for the first time because all travel lines in the world served there, a fitting symbol of how international the Adventist movement had become during its fifty-five years of organized life.

Although Lida Scott did not feel well enough to attend a major church meeting, she still took a keen interest in the developing Los Angeles campus and its students.

"I received a very kind and appreciative letter from the medical students who are occupying the girls' dormitory, and I expect to reply soon and send them a picture of Helen which I have just had enlarged from a Kodak picture I took of her at Asbury Park. I think it is the best I have of her, though the face is not as good as I should like. I think, however, it is a sweet picture, very characteristic and natural. I am not saying anything about the name, Helen Scott Cottage—I'm not to blame if the name sticks, am I?"

Progress was the keynote of the Los Angeles campus now.

"Marguerite [a young woman aiding Lida Scott in her New Jersey home] and I think it is remarkable how quickly the buildings go up," Mrs. Scott continued. "I was surprised that you expect to have patients in the first unit of the hospital by this time. It must be a busy place, and intensely interesting to watch the Administration Building and the Women's Surgical Building hurrying toward completion. I was interested also in what you say about the dispensary clinic doing so well, and how quickly the 15 and 25-cent fees counted up in your hydrotherapy department. I want to congratulate you on your progress and success, and am so glad that the outside local physicians are sympathetic and helpful, and speak so well of the institution to such men as Dr. Colwell."

Dr. Magan was on top of his fund-raising work.

"Let me thank you here for the *Autobiography of Doctor Trudeau*, a book that I have wanted since I saw your copy of it at Madison," she wrote. "I expect to start reading it very soon, and I know I shall enjoy it. It may be I shall get Mr. Scott to read it aloud evenings, as we like to read some book together at that time. It was very kind to think of giving me just the very book I wanted."

One of the first Madison College students to go on to Loma Linda as a medical student was in her thoughts.

"I am glad you wrote to me as you did about Mr. [Julius] Schneider. I know that he is a hard, persevering worker, and have feared that he would not be able to hold out. I have just sent him a check for $50, a gift outright. This is not from my educational fund, as that has been very much overdrawn, but I just could not resist giving him a lift even if I do have to sacrifice some other interest. I forgot at the time what you said about sending the money on to you, so please pardon me that I sent it direct to him. I am glad you are keeping your eye on these worthy young men. While you cannot give them much financial aid yourself, you certainly do give them the sympathy they need, and put yourself out a great deal in their behalf, --and sympathy means so much when discouragement is knocking at the door. I'm sure these young men feel that they have in you a real, true friend. Always feel free, please, to tell me about these cases when you feel impressed. If I cannot do anything I will let you know, for I never have to be worried that you may take a refusal as a personal slight for you are too broad minded for that."

And then there always was the subject of money.

"I am writing to Brother Bowen concerning the $5,000, which I still have on interest at Loma Linda. I have told him to pay me $3,000 now, and to leave $2,000 there at 4 percent."

Magan clearly gave her satisfaction, even when he wasn't sure he was doing so.

"You speak of these little trips you had costing a good deal, but, Doctor Magan, they were well worth the price since so much has been accomplished for the school. You know our denominational men are spending large sums of money in traveling expenses, sending our ministers from the Atlantic to the Pacific, and from the Pacific to the Atlantic, from New Jersey to Florida; the president of the New Jersey Conference becomes president of the Florida Conference, and the president of the Florida Conference comes back to take the presidency of the New Jersey Conference; a teacher from South Lancaster Academy, where she is perfectly happy in her work, is taken clear across the country to Pacific Union College where she is a long time getting adjusted; and two teachers from Walla Walla College were sent back to South Lancaster, unsettling them all—of course, and what has been accomplished? Confusion, it seems to me! We don't mind paying for something. I do feel when you have been oscillating between Los Angeles and Chicago, and New York and Washington and Nashville, that the trips were well worth while, and God was glorified as results show. So you do not need to apologize because the big things that God has done for Loma Linda have required an outlay of money. It is one thing to obey God and another thing to obey men, and I am glad that in your case the Lord was leading, as even Elder Evans, Knox and Daniells agree, as you tell me, that the Lord has given success to the school at a time when it seemed to them it was doomed."

The use of drugs was of concern to her.

"Referring to the unpublished Testimony on drugs, you will find the one I mentioned beginning, 'Put no confidence in drug medication, etc.' on page 45 of those Testimonies collected at Madison by Brother Spaulding. Other references which I have been reading lately, and with which you are no doubt familiar, are as follows: Pages 7, 30, 45, 137, 258, 320, of the same book. I also read the following, urging a revival of teaching the use of herbs as a medicine. I was pleased to find this as I have been wondering for years if Sister White had never said anything about this in her writings. It is on page 137. I have wondered whether the Lord would not inspire someone to revive this lost art of the simple, old-fashioned use of herbs for the treatment of ailments. Doctors are destined to become scarce, and dangerous transportation will shut people up to themselves so that they will need to know how to get along without the doctor. Who is going to teach them?"[1]

The opening of the White Memorial Hospital with dignitaries from the church and community attending on April 21, 1918, pleased Mrs. Scott.

"And so the dedication is an accomplished fact," she wrote to him on May 2, 1918. "We were thinking of you on that day and praying that the Lord would bless, and when I saw in the paper that there was an earthquake in California I wondered if all the people gathered together at the dedication appreciated one story buildings! It seemed to me that the Lord was speaking through that earthquake an approval of your plans. I surely would have been at the dedication if it had been possible."[2]

Prominent participants in that service included J. W. Christian, president of the Pacific Union; F. T. Woodman, mayor of Los Angeles; Dr. E. R. Maloney, A. G. Daniells, and E. E. Andross along with twenty members of the General Conference Committee. "The excellent equipment of the school has now enabled it to attain rating as a medical school of the

'B' class," stated the news account of the dedication. "Only a few heavily endowed or State schools have the A-class rating."[3]

Lida Scott had been through a low point in her life but now seemed to be on her way back to normal as she divided her time between New Jersey and Madison, Tennessee. "Day before yesterday Dr. Hoffer extracted two more teeth. There was a good deal of pus. I have felt like a different woman since and there is every indication that I am going to build up fast now.

"There are a fine lot of influential people here as patients now, and this has been true ever since I have been here," she wrote from the Madison Rural Sanitarium. "I shall expect to be more prompt in my replies now since I am so much better. I shall no doubt be here for some time yet."[4]

"I was very glad indeed to receive your long letter of May 2nd, which I found awaiting me on my return from Walla Walla," Dr. Magan wrote to Mrs. Scott on May 27, 1918. "It looks as if the hand of God was mightily working in behalf of our Medical College. Elder Daniells and others of our leading men are pressing me to do everything in my power to get up more buildings and to get the School in shape so we can enter the A Grade next winter. You see next winter there is to be a 'final' visitation of all the medical colleges in the country by the Council on Medical Education and the Association of American Medical Colleges, which two practically represent the Government at this time. Five men will make this visitation, and will be the most thorough thing of the kind ever undertaken. If we can get into the A Grade then our case is settled forever, that is as long as God wants our people to prepare medical missionaries for the world. I have now been urged to complete this plant as rapidly as I can get hold of the money. The brethren want me to put up the building which will contain class rooms, kitchen, dining rooms, and laboratories at once, and I am doing everything in my power to get money for this. I have also been urged to put up the building for the maternity and children's hospital."[5]

Things were moving forward as 1918 reached its midpoint. The hospital was an accomplished fact. His old rivalries with the General Conference leaders seemed settled, and the church members were generous.

"Somehow or other I have had a premonition for sometime that God wanted things completed and done here, and the School put in a place where it could do good strong work forever," he wrote to Mrs. Scott. "You know I have thought so much of late of Matthew 25:6, At *midnight* there was a cry made, Behold the bridegroom cometh, *go ye out* to meet him.' It is always at midnight that the Lord comes into our lives, and it has been abundantly proven so in our medical missionary work, and more than that, we never will meet the Lord, or meet his mind in anything, unless we 'go out' to meet him. We have got to venture things. I do not know how I am going to get the money for these buildings, but God is moving upon hearts, and there are some big things in prospect which I hope in time will materialize. I have full faith, however, that God is in this whole thing, and that I must press on. It will take considerable money, but there never was a time when our people had as much money as they have now, and there never was a time when they were so willing to give it. I wish you might have been in the meeting at General Conference when $250,000 in cash and pledges was given for missions. It was all done in about 20 minutes, without any pulling or hauling to get it. God was working.

"We are endeavoring to start a number of reforms. We are putting in the cafeteria plan for our patients; we are also doing this at Loma Linda and Glendale. Dr. Sutherland and I talked this over when I was there last summer, and he thought it was a great thing, and I think felt very favorable to putting it in at Madison. We have already been trying it at Glendale, and it works wonderfully. The patients like it, and it is far better for the institution. There is less waste and we make more money; and on account of the present necessity for food conservation, now is the time to do it.

"We are very short of nurses, but expect a large class next fall, also a number of people to take special training in laboratory work, matrons' work, and head nurses' work. I have never seen such a spirit among our students and nurses to do things for the Lord as there is now. God is certainly moving upon their hearts by His Holy Spirit.

"I have to be in Chicago June 11th to attend a conference, called by the Surgeon General of the United States Army, of the dean of medical colleges to settle a number of important questions; and I will run down to Tennessee from there, and hope to have a good visit with you. I hope you won't be gone before then."[6]

Dr. Magan would have other good news to share with her.

"I do not know whether or not I told you in a previous letter that Dr. Truman is with us here now. He is a great help. He is such a godly, conscientious man—one who prays with people. I think I told you that Elder Elderson from South Africa was here and that we are now getting men and women who are appointed to foreign mission work. Elder Anderson is our Bible teacher and does excellent work, and all of our people love him very dearly. We have also been very blessed in getting a splendid young man, Brother Myron Lysinger, as Business Manager. He has been at St. Helena and Loma Linda for a long time but felt anxious to get away from these places, the spirit of our work here attracting him to us. He works so harmoniously and is willing to do anything, even to going into the kitchen and scraping pots and kettles on Sabbath to help out in a pinch. He has got a little of the Madison spirit in him that way. We have had a hard time here before in regard to buying groceries, vegetables, etc., for the house, drugs for the Dispensary, and general supplies. A man came once a week from Loma Linda to do this buying for us. He did it very badly and it made a great deal of trouble, as we could not get the things we wanted for our patients or the proper supplies for our medical department. Mr. Lysinger is attending to all of this and our department heads are getting better pleased and things are going easier. He has just been in here talking to me and telling me about getting him a little Ford delivery wagon and runabout thing so that he can go down and get our groceries and vegetables and stuff early in the morning, and then use the thing later in the day for handling convalescent patients and things of that kind if we need to, so we are working and praying now over this. We have never had any car of any kind here. My car had been used for everything, but of course it was not suited for delivery work. I expect we shall have to get something pretty soon as I understand Ford is going to quit making commercial vehicles immediately and his works will be devoted entirely to Government orders."[7]

Better relations with the church leaders looked hopeful.

"I do not suppose it will be necessary for me to tell you much about the Council here, as Brother Sutherland will tell you all about it. It is by far the best meeting of the kind I have ever attended. Spiritually it had its limitations, which he will detail to you, but it was so different from the one of last year that I could hardly believe I was facing the same men in the same audience chamber that I did just one year ago when my good friend I. H. Evans condemned me to the denomination bowwows for all my heresies for wanting Seventh-day Adventist nurses to care for poor, wounded men in France; for wanting to operate a special school of intensive nurses' training for our young men who have to go into the army; for wanting to give a special course of training for graduate Adventist nurses so they can be of more service to the Government; for wanting to get up a base hospital, etc. etc. The movie reel had certainly changed and my doctrines were all orthodox this time and everything I asked for and desired was unanimously voted. More than that, we got the General Conference Committee to forgive the hospital the debt of $20,000 which the committee loaned us last November. I feel mighty good over this; it will save me a lot of hard work."[8]

The building program for the Los Angeles campus was on track.

"On my return from Palo Alto, San Francisco and St. Helena yesterday I found your good letter of the 18th acknowledging mine of the 8th relative to the $6,000 which you so kindly gave on the Service Building," Dr. Magan wrote to Mrs. Scott. "We are pushing things ahead pretty fast now on the Service Building, and if we can get the material are almost ready to start on the chapel building. It will be a great comfort to us when we can get into the Service Building and that will give us classrooms, kitchens, etc. I am glad to say that Brother Drake tells me that he is going to get the building completed for the amount, which he estimated. I hate to have buildings run over in cost.

"The buildings are almost completed for our school of Army Nursing for the drafted men. They are at Loma Linda and not at Los Angeles, and we expect to have the school running now in the course of a few days. I am sure that this will bring comfort to many a mother's heart to know that her boy can have this training and that it will put them in a line of work more suited to her faith when he is in the Army than some other line into which he might fall were it not for this."[9]

This comment referred to the church's appropriating funds to organize a school for intensive nurses' training at Loma Linda for young men subject to the draft so they could take up medical service once they entered the armed forces.[10]

And other people were investing their money in the medical school.

"You will be interested to know that a patient at Hinsdale, a Mrs. Rhodes, who is not an Adventist, has given us most of the money for an adding machine and in all probabilities is going to give us the rest. It is wonderful the way the Lord is bringing people to our help. They know that we are working for the poor and they love us and help us on our road a bit. The other day, I had as a present a nice electric blanket from old Sister Learned in Glendale and with some other little donations we got our money together to get a desk for Dr. Lillian."[11]

Dr. Magan remembered the people who had made it all possible.

"I can never tell you, Sister Scott, how much I appreciate all you have done for us on this matter of the hospital, and also for all you have done for us at Madison," he wrote to her on July 18, 1918. "Truly, God raised you up to help these two lines of work in perilous times of great need. There are three women in this world who stand out in my mind as saviors of God's cause when in perilous places more than any others, -- Josephine Gotzian, May Covington, and Lida F. Scott. Over and over again things would have come to an end for us if it had not been that the Lord brought you good souls to our rescue and I feel assured that in the Kingdom of Heaven there will be bright stars in your crown for all this work. You have made many and great sacrifices and I love you for them all and pray that God will keep you in health of body, in strength of soul and sweetness of spirit to the day of His coming. I am so very glad you are feeling so much better. You have had a long, hard, discouraging time of it."[12]

The *Review and Sabbath Herald* also had good things to say about the medical school. A report of the North American Division Medical Department noted that the B rating had come based "solely upon the merits of the school" and also that in Washington, D.C., "one of the most difficult cities in which to obtain recognition," one of its graduates "had the honor of receiving the highest grade of any applicant at any examination during the entire year."[13]

Meade MacGuire, field secretary for the General Conference Missionary Volunteer Department, wrote that he had been impressed with the spiritual atmosphere at the Loma Linda medical college as well as its graduates now part of the Lord's work. "I do not hesitate to say that I know of no nobler, more earnest, or more consecrated workers in our cause than are these young people."[14]

Then, when the Grade A rating seemed within reach, World War I again intervened and threatened to undo all that Magan had accomplished during the past two years. In September, the government announced that the U.S. Army would exempt only students in a medical school with a Students' Army Training Corps (SATC) program, something the College of Medical Evangelists did not have.

"I have just returned from Palo Alto where I had a visit with Ray Lyman Wilbur, who is president of Leland Stanford University and also is one of the big men of the Government in this Students' Army Training Corps business," Magan wrote to Mrs. Scott. "He treated me splendidly and wrote out a great telegram and sent it to Washington recommending that we be put on the Government list for a Students' Army Training School. I also had a good time at St. Helena. If we get this Students' Army Training Corps Unit we will have their premedical students down here."[15]

General Conference leaders feared that such a situation would jeopardize the non-combatancy status of Adventist servicemen. The College of Medical Evangelists administration worked out a compromise plan of having students on the Loma Linda campus drill for six hours a week at nearby Redlands University, and the Los Angeles students do the same at Occidental College, but the General Conference refused to allow any students to join SATC, even though they would go into the army as physicians and not carry weapons once they finished school. The flu epidemic spreading worldwide in 1918, a public health crisis killing many people, then forced Dr. Magan to bed during the most serious of these negotiations with church and governmental leaders. Dr. Evans had to stand in for him.

Matters ended in an impasse, with draft boards bringing up the names of the medical students for induction into the armed forces. If they left for the U.S. Army, the school would close forever.

To encourage him through this serious crisis, Lida Scott wrote in October of 1918, "A few days ago I was culling my files and I reread a letter from you dated in 1916 when you were worried about the rerating of Loma Linda and Dr. Colwell was so discouraging in everything he said. And yet when everything looked the very darkest you reached the conclusion that the Lord was about to do great things for the medical school. You based this on your faith in God's Word in the Bible and Testimonies. It was so interesting to reread those pages in the light of today and to see how the Lord honored your faith and those associated with you. It is a page in sacred history. He will surely finish that work he has begun, and is quite able to work out all the present problems as well as he did those of the past."[16]

The November 11, 1918, armistice ending World War I saved the school.[17]

By December, things seemed back to normal, at least for the time being.

"My dear Sister Scott," Dr. Magan wrote, "I was so glad to get your kind letter of December 4. I am picking up some after the influenza but I feel it yet and the strain we have been through here in the last two years seems to be telling on me. I wish I could get away from it all for a month or two but I do not see any way to do it. I am teaching nearly all of the Medicine now to the Junior Class and doing quite a lot of work in the Hospital and some outside practice, beside the general work that comes to the office of the Dean of a large school like this.

"We have certainly had a terrible time here with the Influenza. We have had a very large number of cases here at the hospital and some of the most fearful pneumonia cases I have ever seen. God has greatly blessed in the care of these cases. The Los Angeles County Hospital has lost 25 percent of their cases and we have lost only something over four percent of ours; in fact, I think our later series of cases will bring it down to about three percent. This certainly speaks well for God's methods of treatment.

"Katherine Magan, Wellesley's wife, has had it quite badly lately. She is now on the mend again but she suffered a great deal, poor girl, and is not out of it yet. We have had numbers of entire families down with it all at the same time. In one case the entire family died, one after the other. It is distressing and indeed seems like [a] plague of the last days.

"Shaen has escaped the influenza so far. He comes down to see us every Sabbath nearly. He starts out afoot from Loma Linda and picks up rides as he can for the 65 miles."

The Los Angeles campus was taking shape.

"Well, I have all the money together now for our chapel. I feel very thankful for that. When we get it up we will have some place to meet and worship. The next building to be gone after is the maternity and children's building. We have every bed full now all the time and you will be thankful to hear that in spite of all the predictions which Elder Knox made that this place would run behind $50,000 a year, we have paid every bill out of our own earnings to date. I feel that the Lord has been very good to us in this."

Even the enrollment was looking up.

"You will be glad to know that we have more young men in the first year medical class this year than in all our other classes all together. God has certainly blessed us in this. Did I tell you that I got a bill through the General Conference Council in Washington which provides for the attaching of a lady physician to the office of the General Conference Medical Secretary, whose chief business it is to go around to our schools and sanitariums and interest young women students and nurses in becoming physicians?"[18]

And then the year of 1918 closed with another major victory. Dr. Magan would benefit the school by rising in the medical profession.

"You will also be interested, I am sure, to know that another big fight of long time standing here has been fought and won. For years we were not allowed any representation upon the Staff of the Los Angeles County Hospital. The Los Angeles Hospital is the largest in the United States except Cook County in Chicago, and physicians on the Staff were of great value to the medical schools in this city on account of the teaching facilities offered and involved. Recently things have swung around and the

Board of Supervisors of this County made me a permanent member of the Governing Medical Board of the Hospital, which is composed of eight men, including myself. From a medical standpoint this is considered a very high honor, but it also carries with it the right to appoint a number of men on the Staff of the Hospital, and this is the thing which is of such great value to us. The Lord is certainly putting this place on the map."[19]

The great personalities in the drama

They brought Adventism into the big leagues.

Percy Magan entered the medical profession in mid life and went on to become a consummate educator, fund raiser, administrator and diplomat. Seventh-day Adventist medical work achieved high standing through his efforts.

Edward A. Sutherland started out as the senior partner of Percy Magan at their schools in Michigan and Tennessee. When Magan went to Los Angeles on his own, Sutherland helped him with crucially needed financial support through his access to the personal fortune of Lida Funk Scott.

Lida Scott, a new convert to Adventism, needed healing as much as Sutherland and Magan needed money. Each satisfied the other.

Arthur G. Daniells, one of the most successful General Conference presidents the Seventh-day Adventist Church ever had, could never work comfortably with prominent medical professionals like John Harvey Kellogg, Percy T. Magan or EA. Sutherland.

Percy T. Magan looks very distinguished in his later photographs, an elder statesman of the Seventh-day Adventist Church and American Medical Association.

A New Era Opens

The Year 1919

"I congratulate you on your appointment on the Governing Medical Board of the Los Angeles County Hospital," Lida Scott wrote to Dr. Magan on January 17, 1919. "That I should think will be of immense value to us. How wonderful is the God of Israel."[1]

Another need then grabbed her attention.

"A letter just received from Dr. Sutherland lays before me the necessity of your attending the Council on Medical Education to be held in Chicago in March," she wrote to him from New Jersey on January 31. "I am glad I am to have a part in it for it strikes me as exceedingly important that you keep closely in touch with these men and I do not understand how any of our leading men can fail to recognize the fact.

"It is splendid to know that the Lord has given the vision to you. This scripture comes to my mind, And I Daniel alone saw the vision: for the men that were with me saw not the vision; but a great quaking fell upon them, so that they fled to hide themselves.' [Daniel 10:7]

"I consider it a great privilege to help and if this check of $200 which I enclose should not be sufficient to accomplish the Lord's purpose please let me know for there is still a balance in the educational fund.

"The Lord has given to every man his work and He has given this part of the work to me I am glad to say. Oh, it is a glorious thing to have a part in our medical evangelical work.

"Trust we shall see you when you come east. I am expecting to return to Madison about the first of March."[2]

"I cannot tell you how much I appreciated your kind letter of January 31 in which you refer to Dr. Sutherland's letter concerning the necessity of my attending the Council on Medical Education," Dr. Magan replied to her on February 13. "I greatly appreciate your check for $200. This will give me enough money so that I can attend this Council and do some other things that need to be done badly. I am in hopes that I can also get down to New York so as to talk a few matters over with you."[3]

In another letter, he referred to this Council on Medical Education as being a "big meeting."[4]

Though Dr. Magan was on his way to being on a first-name basis with the Mayo Clinic medical specialists, he seemed to be having trouble making medical missionary work part of the General Conference program.

"Things are going well here but I am having lots of troubles," he wrote. "It is so hard to do in the machine the things which one can do so easily out of it. Miss Mallory and I laughed quite joyously at the scripture which you so aptly quoted... [from the book of Daniel] "Certainly these texts describe two classes of Adventists beautifully: Men who do not see the vision are certainly subject to a great quaking and they always flee and hide themselves. I think I shall have to steal this text from you and make it the subject of what I believe will be a cracking good sermon."[5]

Conflicts with his General Conference superiors were apparently not yet over.

"I have not any sympathy upon the part of our leading brethren for a strong work in building up this place on the basis of the Spirit of Prophecy," he wrote to her later in the year. "The first fight was to get something started at all in order to insure to our people a denominational medical school. You know well the struggle we had at the General Conference Council in Loma Linda in 1915 when the Hospital was born, and I am sure you will remember my letters to you relative to the struggle again at the General Conference Council in the fall of 1916 in Washington when the brethren voted not to build the Hospital, even although a year before they had voted to build it, and when they voted only to give two years of medical work and to let the students go to worldly schools for the rest of their educating. The next struggle I had in my hands was to get buildings for this place. First of all only half a block of land was bought and I was forbidden to purchase any more and was told that all the money must be saved for one large concrete building before anything could be done. Had I let myself be throttled in this manner there would have been no College of Medical Evangelists today. God knows the truth whereof I speak. Under tremendous stress Brother Burden, Sister Gotzian, Mrs. Kittle and I bought the other half of the block upon which we are now located, taking the responsibility of paying for it ourselves. For this I was severely criticized, but I felt that we must have enough land so that we could put up our buildings on a simple cottage style, and God has blessed in this and our buildings now stand as a monument to that experience and are in harmony with what has been written in the Spirit of Prophecy in regard to Seventh-day Adventist buildings. I do not know how much you have ever read these Testimonies but they are very plain and clear. Even now we are bitterly criticized from Washington for the simple bungalow type of our buildings, particularly by the son of your old friend and enemy, Elder Miller. I refer to Dr. Harry Miller.

"Just at present I am confronted with the cry that the medical school is growing too large. I was taken upon the green carpet at the Camp meeting at Orange, California, by Elder Knox and by the President of this Union Conference and told that absolutely the school ought not to go beyond 25 students to a class. Our freshman class this year, I expect, will be about 50 members, and I have ample information to make clear to me that this idea is being preached all over the field. At the same time, I have been forbidden to solicit money in the Pacific Union Conference and practically from the entire United States. However, I do not take that to heart very seriously and intend to go ahead and do the best I can."[6]

His years of working with Dr. Sutherland in developing Madison College had been "self-supporting," meaning they could follow the Spirit of Prophecy directions without any administrative restraint. Things were different at Loma Linda.

"The young men in the Medical College have never been in the atmosphere that we have at Madison, and at their age in life, and under the tremendous stress that they are working under, it is going to take a Herculean effort to get things turned in the manner that the Lord wants them turned. This part of the work is now the great burden of my soul. At Madison there was a whole company devoted to certain principles. Here I feel I am practically alone battling in large part a faculty that have never done anything on the basis of faith in God and who have always worked in the old regular routine way. I have felt that some of my old friends thought I have not gotten enough workers out into the field in a real self-sacrificing way for the cause of God, but I do not think that these realize what has been accomplished and what we have had to meet. It is only two years ago last January that I came to Los Angeles and began building the Dispensary building. I have had to gather the money, attend to the planning of the buildings, fight off the brethren and until recently was my own Business Manager, run a cafeteria for the students because the Board would not take one cent's responsibility in the matter, and endeavor to build up a clientele of patients and students, as well as to organize a Faculty. The War came and you know something of the difficulties which it brought into the work at Madison. With us the difficulties were far greater than Madison had to face as the very life of the school was at stake. Then came the Influenza to which all our energies had to be devoted as long as that dire plague lasted. Now I am endeavoring that this coming school year shall mark a new era in the work here and I feel very much alone in the effort which I see must be put forth. Over and over again I comfort myself with the words of David when he wrote, 'The Lord will perfect that which concerneth him.' I know that God is in what we are trying to do here but I feel that our friends will have to be a little lenient with us and give us a little time. Two years is not very long in which to make so many reforms as have to be made in this place.

In 1915 when I first came out here there were just four students in the freshman class. It has taken no small effort and no small amount of prayer to change the sentiment of the field so that now we have 50. Undoubtedly in doing what we have done we have made a good many mistakes and failures, but I often think of those words in the Psalms where David writes, 'Unto Thee, O Lord, do I lift up my soul. Oh my God, I trust in Thee. Let me not be ashamed, let not thine enemy triumph over me. Yea, let none that wait on thee be ashamed. Let them be ashamed which transgress without cause.'"[7] [psalms25:1-3]

He knew where to go for strength.

"Many things about the work here worry me a great deal and I long for Ed, [Dr. E.A. Sutherland at Madison] as I have no one here whom I feel that I know the way I do him and there is no one associated with me here who gets in the harness the way he and I used to be able to get under it together," he later wrote.[8]

Dr. Magan assumed that doing what he regarded as right based on his study would vindicate him even if it did cause tension with the church leaders for the time being.

"Evidently the Bible recognizes two kinds of transgressions. There are those who transgress willfully and just because they want to. These are the ones of whom it is written that they 'transgress without cause.' There are others who have a cause for their transgressing. They are in hard places and doing the best they can and God recognizes this and records it in a totally different manner to what he does the other. This is clearly seen in the life of David when he sinned with Bathsheba and when he numbered the people. He transgressed without cause. But when he went to Achish, King of Gath, and pretended he was a lunatic, while the thing that he did was not right, he was not transgressing without a cause. He was in a hard place and God knew it and never punished him for that, and again, when he went to Amalek and told him that the King had commanded him a business and had told him not to let any man know what it was—while this was a lie, nevertheless, God never punished him for that for God knew the straits he was in."⁹

How he missed his partner from Madison.

"I would give anything if Dr. Sutherland could be here with me for awhile, but that seems impossible. In building up this work practically alone I fear greatly at times that I will make grave mistakes and put the wrong mold upon it, but God only knows why some one who has a vision of this thing has not been sent to work with me and why I have had to stand here so much alone."¹⁰

His vision for his students just did not square with that of the church leadership.

"And now when I try to get our boys into the work, and when they are willing to go, then I find myself up against almost insurmountable difficulties and red tape upon the part of the General Conference. If it is not one thing it is another. However, the tide seems to be turning a bit in that. No one knows the struggles I had with Ralph Smith to keep him true to his promise to God to get him to go to Mexico. The letters he received from Washington utterly discouraged him, and now I feel that I must stand by him that he is down there and help him get on his feet.

"Well, I want you to pray for me for I am in a hard place. Dr. Evans is good but he has no vision of this thing and he has been away all summer and will not be back until school opens."¹¹

Drs. Newton Evans and Percy Magan proved to be an effective team to lead the College of Medical Evangelists, with Dr. Evans being strong in research and teaching on the Loma Linda campus. Magan did most of the fund raising and was in charge of things at Los Angeles.

"It is splendid that you are not letting the missionary spirit die out during the strenuous years of medical training," Lida Scott wrote to him in encouragement. "That is a happy thought to collect Sister White's old manuscripts, etc, in a little cottage. I am going to try to give something for that cottage if I find it possible. But I am helping enlarge Madison this next year, and I fear my hands will be tied for much further effort.

"The Lord is watching over your work, evidenced in so many ways, of which it is the way the money came to you for the maternity and children's hospital, and the results of Dr. Winterer's visit.

"If the Lord gives me strength, ... I may go to Los Angeles this summer. I am anxious to see what God has wrought."¹²

Then, in getting down to her real motivation in financially supporting the College of Medical Evangelists, she wrote, "I wish some broad-minded young graduate with courage and vision would go to Madison and cooperate with Dr. Sutherland. The work there is growing so big and broad. It would seem help must come. Isn't that new city development significant?"[13]

Here lay her and Dr. Sutherland's vision. The Madison institution was encouraging its students to go into the southeastern United States with only a token Adventist presence and reproduce the Madison model of a school, sanitarium, and farm on one campus. They came up with the word *unit* to describe the actual operation. These units needed physicians to attract patients. These sanitariums provided financial stability as well as medical missionary contact with the community. Several of these units would become Southern Union Conference academies and hospitals in the years to come.

The need for doctors made Dr. Sutherland and Mrs. Scott regard Loma Linda as one of their family of institutions. Lida Scott therefore wanted to help students willing to work in the underprivileged South as trained medical missionaries.

"Now about Miss Hennessy. I will pay one half her expenses the first year provided the other half is raised," she offered. "Please keep this on file in case someone forgets.

"I have here a young lady staying with me this winter, Miss Lingham, whom I brought with me from Madison to rest up as she has suffered nervously from overwork. She has a splendid physique and will be vigorous in mind and body when she is herself again. She is one of the most promising young women I have ever known, a graduate of the Framingham Normal School. She is not yet an Adventist but is tremendously interested. She has too tired a head to study much now. She wants to take the nurses' course, or part of it, at Madison then the medical course at Loma Linda. Then she wants to devote her life as self-supporting missionary among the mountaineers. I expect to help her through college, but this will be a couple of years yet, I suppose, before I have this expense to meet.

"Next year I am willing to pay the half of the expenses of a second promising young woman, especially favoring one who is burdened for mountain work in the south. But more of this later.

"I will offer $300 a year for four years in behalf of training women medically for our southern highland work. What do you think of some such plan? Can one or two women be found with this southern burden that will need the whole or half of her expenses paid for here?"[14]

Magan was happy to help his friends in the South.

"Thank you very much for your kind word relative to Miss Hennessy; namely, that you will pay one-half of her expenses for the first year provided the other half is raised," Dr. Magan replied to her. "That is very good of you and I believe you are helping a most worthy girl. It may be that some time you will be down in Washington and will be able to see Miss Hennessy there for yourself. I was greatly pleased with her appearance and she has the most excellent recommendations.

"I am interested in all you write about Miss Ungham. I do not think I have ever met her but I trust her stay with you will result in her being a good Seventh-day Adventist. I understood that Miss Mencke was to be with you. Am I right in this? I am glad you are going to help Miss Lingham through school and I am thankful to know that you will be willing to pay half of the expenses of a second promising young woman, especially if she is favorable to work amongst the mountaineers of the South. Have you any one in mind? I have a young woman here, a Miss Dale, whom I am intending to help through if I can get the help for her. She has been a schoolteacher and is a most godly, plain going girl. Her father is not an Adventist and the girl has had a hard time of it. I have never talked to her especially about the South but she is the cut of a girl I think would do well there.

"I am glad you like my thought of collecting Sister White's old manuscripts, library, etc., in a nice little cottage here," he continued. "I do not know how soon my vision on this will materialize. There are so many, many things to be done and sometimes I feel altogether unequal to the task. Still, in spite of all our trials, things are prospering and God is blessing us. You have been a mighty good friend to us here and I do not want you to feel that you have to strain yourself to give every time we have a need, so just let this little cottage rest and do not give it further thought and I will see how we will come along.

Fund raising was still going well.

"We have started work on our church and I have all the money raised to pay for it. We have turned this money over to the Southern California Conference and they are building it in cooperation with us. I do not have to worry any further about it. In a few months I hope we will be able to start the maternity and children's building. God has certainly been good to us over this. As I wrote you before, all the money has been subscribed for it but is not all in hand yet, but will be soon, I believe.

"I am so thankful to know that there is a little chance of our seeing you in Los Angeles this summer. I do not know of any one we will be more thankful to see than yourself.

"I have written Dr. E. A. Sutherland and begged him to come out here and give some talks to our students on the work in the South. I am sure if he comes that he will be able to get some good workers."[15]

Lida Scott seemed satisfied.

"Your two letters as usual were full of inspiration," she wrote to Dr. Magan on June 22. "I have read them over two or three times, and do appreciate your taking time to give me in detail the Acts of God in the development of our medical work. How in connection with the Students' Army Training Corps you were by faith warned of things not seen as yet and moved with fear, and God guarded you as was afterwards made clear by the flat failure of that movement; and how also the school chose rather to suffer affliction with the principles of God than to enjoy the pressures of recognition of the world for a season, and God honored your faith by taking you through the sea and causing the waters to close upon the University of Southern California which was trying to destroy His chosen school; and how He has taken care of the recognition as we are told He would.

"I am very much interested in all you wrote about the good honest men among the great physicians of the town who love these principles," Mrs. Scott continued, "how they are anxious to get on our staff, Dr. Rhea Smith, Dr. Charles Browning, Dr. Lettice, and Dr. Leighton. Dr. Bryson I suppose is the Pharaoh in this case. We all hope and pray that the principles given us on the drug question, hydrotherapy, diet, etc., will never suffer depreciation. God can bless only right principles, and He, with us, though we be ever so weak, if we be obedient, will more than counterbalance the influence of any number of great men. Our only safety in these days, when we have the sympathy and cooperation of the world, is to 'be strong and very courageous.' I feel that I have not prayed for you all as I should. We should each pray that God will help our medical workers to feel very small in His sight."[16]

She then turned to her desire to build up the Lord's work in the South.

"How is it that no graduates from Loma Linda have yet felt the burden to connect with the southern work? What is wrong that so many are anxious to go into private practice? I understand that Dr. Thomason has set a wonderful example, making a great personal sacrifice by throwing in his lot with you accepting a small salary. What is going to bring that spirit of self-sacrifice among our students so that some will even dare to trust God for their pay as you and Dr. Sutherland have done here at this place for so many years? Cannot something be done to awaken in them that spirit? We do so need medical evangelists here, but then, you know all about that. We hope to hear soon that the attention of many will be turned this way. Perhaps your new Bible teacher, Elder H. J. Waldorf, will help them to see what the Testimonies say about the South as a training camp for foreign service."[17]

"You ask how it is that no graduates from Loma Linda have yet felt the burden to connect with the Southern work. Brother Sutherland has never called for but two," Dr. Magan replied. "Dr. Swift went down there, who, since getting out of the Army has gone to our Sanitarium at Walla Walla, Washington, and Dr. Alma Larson. She willingly gave up her position at the Portland Sanitarium to go to Madison, but as possibly Dr. Sutherland has told you, she has had some kind of a nervous breakdown and is sick in Minnesota. Just when she will be able to go and take up her work I do not know. She felt a deep burden for the southern work. Possibly you may remember that she was with us in Madison years ago. In the old days when I was in the state of Minnesota I found her and got her to go to Madison to help us in the work. She took the nurses' course there and was a very efficient girl. Afterward a Sister Peck in Minnesota, whose husband is not an Adventist but who has been very kind to our people, agreed to put her through medical college and after she was through I wired Dr. Sutherland, asking if he did not want her for Madison, as she was willing to go. At that time he had Dr. Swift and felt he could not take on any more help. She then went to Portland, but as stated above, when Brother Sutherland called for her she was more than glad to give up her place there in order to join him. He wrote the other day that until it was settled whether she would be able to come or not he did not feel like calling for anybody else. This covers the Madison phase of the question.

"In regard to others being interested in the Southern Highlands, I think the matter is about this way. Practically none of our students here know much of anything about the work there beyond what I have told them. They have never been there. So many of our students are from California. Not very many of them come from across the continent and their knowledge of the South and its needs is small. I have begged Brother Sutherland to come out here and spend awhile laying the needs of the South before us, and I have no doubt but what he can get some to go back there to engage with him in the work; but someone who has definite propositions as to places that need help and just what can be done, etc., needs to come here from the South and talk to them. I can, of course, talk to them in a general way, but I do not have the close touch with the work there now that I formerly had and consequently cannot lay definite propositions before them as I once could.

"Again, you ask, 'What is wrong that so many are anxious to go into private practice?' I think you must be misinformed on this. Up to the time when our nation entered the War approximately 96 or 98 percent, I have forgotten just which, of the graduates of this school were in our own work. This is a higher percentage by far of laborers definitely placed in the cause than is held by any other school amongst us. I have never known of another school in our midst having put as many workers in the field, proportionately, as Loma Linda has. When the War came, of course, it threw everything into hard shape. Practically every one of our young men was taken as medical officers in the Army and that situation is not entirely straightened out yet. There were 22 in that class and I think on the whole we have much to be thankful for concerning the way they have done.

"For instance, Dr. Birkenstock is in Edinburgh getting ready to return to South Africa, the field from which he came. Dr. Frederick Bulpitt is in the work at Loma Linda and Dr. Roos is also at Loma Linda. Dr. Burgeson and his wife, Dr. Edna Burgeson, have gone to Hastings, Nebraska. Dr. Arthur Coyne has charge of our Dispensary. Dr. Hara is in the Japanese work here. Dr. Johnston is entering the service at St. Helena. Dr. Alma Larson was at Portland and when able will go to Madison. Dr. Clarence Nelson will be out of the Army in September and then join us here. Dr. Stump has gone to the Portland, Oregon Sanitarium. Dr. Ruth Temple is in the colored work here amongst her own people. That makes 11 out of the 22 definitely doing what they can in the work. Of the others, Dr. John Bulpitt is sick with tuberculosis. Dr. Edwards has lain at death's door for months from a lung abscess following the Influenza. Dr. Richard Elvin was taken in the Canadian Army and is only just now getting out. Dr. Walter Lenker is just closing up his internship at the San Bernardino County Hospital. Dr. Maker has not finished with his Army internship at the Los Angeles Hospital. Dr. Mabel Butka has been sick and is now waiting for the return of her husband, Dr. Hersel Butka, from France. He takes charge of our laboratory here in Los Angeles and she in all probability will help him, which can fairly count her as the twelfth in the work. Wellesley was asked by the Pacific Union Conference to take Dr. Abbott's place at Covina until someone else could be found for it. He and Katherine will probably go to China as soon as the way opens for them to do that. Dr. Schlotthauer is a German and a most peculiar fellow and the brethren did not feel that he would fit very well into any of our institutions. He is in private practice. Dr. Claude Steen is in private practice and ought not to be. Dr. Morfan has apostatized from the faith altogether. Dr. Feldkamp is in private practice and ought not to be. This covers the list and I cannot help but feel that the showing is remarkably good under the circumstances.

"Of the class that has just graduated there are only five members and they are distributed as follows: Dr. Amyes goes to Scotland to get British recognition so he can return to his home in New Zealand and labor there. Dr. Falconer goes for a year to St. Helena and then joins Dr. Selmon in Shanghai, China. Dr. Earl Gardner interns here at the White Memorial for a year and then if present plans carry will go to Malaysia. Dr. Bummel has only just come into the truth, and in fact, was not an Adventist when he came to us from the University of California the middle of the school year just closed. He will be with us for a year at the White Memorial trying to learn more about the truth and our ways of doing things and what his future beyond that will be I do not know. Dr. Scoles is going out on a contract practice.

"Now, Sister Scott, some may think that our boys are not being very true to this work, but I think I can safely challenge any Adventist school on the face of the earth to show a much better record than this, and this in the face of the fact that more temptations to go into worldly work and practice favor our medical boys than any other class of student graduates amongst us.

"Our medical evangelistic class has never been composed of really first class students. To be sure, there have always been some very fine people in that class, but many of them were not the very best timber by any means. However, practically all of that class this year is now in the work, and a number of them are in a self-supporting work. If Ed could only come out here and talk with them I am sure we could get up some money to pay the fares of some of them and get them to the South, but it is difficult to get them there when they have never been there and know nothing about it except what I tell them and when I have no definite propositions to put before them.

"Yes, Thomason has set a wonderful example and it is having its effect. I only wish more of our doctors here were doing the way he is."[18]

He was also proud of a ministerial kind of medical missionary to South America whom his school had taken through a crash course.

"I am enclosing in this copy of a letter which I received from Brother Orley Ford who is now one of our missionaries high up on the Andes

Mountains in Peru," he wrote to Mrs. Scott later in the summer. "This young man is a minister and a teacher and was sent here by the General Conference to get some training in medical work before he went to his field of labor. I think we had him and his young wife here for three months—possibly a little more than that, but no great amount of time anyhow. I have always felt that bright young men of this kind could be taught a whole lot in a short time and we pitched in to do our very best on this lad. We worked him in around in all of the departments of the Dispensary, especially Surgery, Medicine and the Eye Department, and his wife worked in Obstetrics and Gynecology. This letter will give you an idea of what he has been able to do. I feel that if this school never did anything more than this kind of work it would be doing a great deal to bless poor people who are sick and who need help."[19]

Dr. Magan's faith was still strong.

"I, too, feel very thankful that God kept us safely through the entire crisis concerning the Students' Army Training Corps. Those were very hard and trying times when Men's wisdom utterly failed. Toward the end of that experience I was down in my bed with the Influenza very sick, and day by day as I lay there it seemed to me a race as to whether the devil would be able to close this school or God could bring the War to an end and get the Armistice signed first. I felt perfectly confident all the way through as to what the outcome would be, but the times were indeed trying for our lads.

"Things are moving along quietly just now. It is vacation and only a few of the young men are there. We are very busy. Every bed is full and the Dispensary is running heavy also. There are so many things, however, to be done, built up and improved and generally gotten in better shape that we feel we cannot slack for a moment. Then again, on the spiritual or real side of things there is so very much to be done. Getting this plant built and things in shape has taken so much of my time that I have not been able to do any other lines what I have wanted to do, but now I hope some of this work will let up a bit and that I shall be able to accomplish some things in a more definite way for the work.

"Did I tell you that I am going to spend awhile with Elder W. C. White this summer getting out a book which will gather together all of the important testimonies which Sister White has given in regard to our medical work from the very first down to the time of her death? We shall endeavor in this book to gather together in different sections all of practical use that has been said on diet; drugs; hydrotherapy; out of door work;

fresh air; right thinking; the importance of nursing work; physicians and their pay; relation of physicians to nurses; relation of workers to institutions; needy fields; our own medical college; worldly medical colleges, etc., etc., and also the Battle Creek apostasy. This will give us something that we shall be able to use as a class textbook and will assist the students in their study. It is quite a big undertaking and I have had quite a long pull with the General Conference people and the Pacific Press in order to get them to publish it; but all of this is agreed to now, excepting that I have to stand good for $500 of the initial expense. I think, however, I shall be able to get this arranged so that it will be paid back to the parties putting it in royalties on the book."[20]

"I am particularly interested in your plans for getting out a book and for collecting Testimonies which relate to our medical work," Lida Scott replied. "I suppose those relating to out-of-door work will include the out of the cities message. This book I am sure will be invaluable to us. I will be glad to give a hundred dollars on the initial expense provided you can arrange to get this paid back in royalties on the book.

"Thank you for explaining to me what is becoming of our medical graduates," she continued. I am glad they nearly all remain in the work. I see the necessity of someone from here making a strong effort to interest them in self-sacrificing, self-supporting work, especially in the South.

"I suppose Doctor Sutherland has written you about our organization here of our Medical Missionary Volunteers which will draw all like minded people into a closer union, and that will give the Madison extension work a stronger backing we hope."[21]

From his end on the West Coast, Magan had the same idea of preparing young people for medical missionary service.

"It is getting near the time when the Medical College will open again for another year and I wanted to write you a little in regard to the matter of the students of whom you told me you would render some aid and assistance," Dr. Magan wrote to her as the summer progressed.

"First of all, there is Miss Ethel Hennessy. You may remember that in your letter of January 17, 1919, to me you told me you would be willing to pay half her way and you asked me to keep your letter on file in case you might forget. I would appreciate it if some time during the next couple of weeks you would send me some money on account for her. Her expenses will probably run in the neighborhood of $450, to $500 for the year. Half of this will be between $225 and $250. It would not be necessary for all of your share of this money to come immediately, but if I could have some of it I would appreciate it. I think we will even have to pay her traveling fare from New York here, which, of course, makes the cost amount up a bit. She is such an exceptionally fine young woman and has been so true to this cause and worked in such a self-sacrificing way for it already that I feel like doing what I can for her.

"You also wrote me in that same letter that you would pay for half the expense of another young woman in addition to Miss Hennessy in medical school, giving the preference to someone, if I could find such a person, who would be interested in medical work in the Southern Highlands. I have a young woman on my list who I have promised to help her whole way through for whom I would like the assistance thus offered by you, and I will make up the other half from elsewhere. This is Miss Mary Dale, of Los Angeles, California. She is one of the most sober, Godly young women I know of. She has charge of the work amongst the children in this part of the country. Her folks are not Adventists so that she has a very hard time of it. She has made up all her premedical work this summer and will be ready to enter this fall. I have talked with her somewhat about going south and she has a burden for that field. Therefore, if you are willing to take my word on her I shall be glad of assistance for her. I do not know of two better young women in the country, or two young women from whom we have more chance of realizing good workers than these two.

"Now while I am at it I want to lay another matter before you. Two years ago there graduated from this school a young doctor by the name of Ralph Smith. He was born in Nebraska and I have known his folks ever since I was a lad myself. He had to go to the Army and had a great experience in regard to the Sabbath but stayed by his guns and came out in good shape. Before the War closed he was a very trusted officer. After he got out he came to me and told me of his great burden to go to Mexico and start work there in medical missionary lines. He met a great deal of discouragement in this. The General Conference brethren agreed to send him and then wrote me afterwards that there was nothing doing. Finally, however, I got them to stand by their part of the contract which was that they would pay the railroad fare of himself and family to Mexico City and give him a small wage for three or four months, after which he would have to shift for himself. The lad had only a few hundred dollars in his pocket but he was determined to go. I borrowed $142.50, which I gave him to buy a few instruments. Please do not think I am asking you to take care of this. I will handle that from some other source altogether, but here is the thing that is troubling me in regard to him now. In fact, I think I will enclose a letter I have just received from him which will give you an idea of the amount and what he is trying to do. You will see by this letter that he wants me to get him $1,000, which he is willing to pay back. This money is to fit up an office for himself. He has some rich uncles and I have written them in his behalf but I do not know whether they will do anything or not. They were very anxious that he go into private practice and make a lot of money. This he absolutely refused to do, so that they are not feeling as kindly toward him as they might be. Now if I get stuck and cannot borrow this money for him from other sources, would you be willing to loan at least a part of it? I will see that he gives you a note and I know the boy is good pay for I have helped him before."[22]

"Your letter of August 8th in which you remind me of my promise to help Miss Ethel Hennessy by paying one half of her expenses and half the expenses of another young lady who has a burden for the Southern field received, and I am glad to enclose a check for $375, $125 for each of the two girls and $125 for Shaen which you will credit to the account of each," she wrote to him. "Thank you for reminding me."[23]

She politely declined to help Ralph Smith but did want to have a part in publishing the book of all Ellen White's writing about medical missionary work.

"I feel rather burdened to push that book you are compiling from Sister White's writings," she said. "That ought to be gotten out by all means and I will pay $100 or more on the initial expense even if I thought it could not be returned, rather than let it fail. I am enclosing check for $150 for that now.

"I realize that you have, and have had, a difficult task before you in standing for the high principles which have been committed to us and I feel that we must get out the book that you proposed no matter what the personal sacrifice is, and for my part I am willing to see it through.

Personally I cannot tell you how much I appreciate the fact that you have set your face like flint though you seem to be all alone there. Your experience is much like that of Elijah, and I believe like him you will see God swing things around where there will be a strong stand made by the students and, we hope, the faculty for the special Testimonies which are the basis upon which the medical college was to be built."[24]

Such a book, *Counsels on Health*, came out in 1923 under the byline of Ellen G. White, with Percy T. Magan writing the preface. The subtitle adds, "and Instruction to Medical Missionary Workers."

Lida Scott moved to Madison, Tennessee, that summer. Her correspondence indicates she had some differences with her fellow believers in the Newark, SDA Church, and handled the situation by transferring her membership to the Madison College Church in 1918. Then in the summer of 1919, she built a small cottage on the campus and made that her home. Her husband remained in New Jersey. She devoted her life and personal fortune to the work of Dr. Sutherland and his associates in the South. Since their great enterprise needed physicians, she also supported Loma Linda and stayed in close touch with Dr. Magan.

"I was so glad to get your letter of August 4 and to know that you have at last been able to move into your little bungalow and that you are now getting settled," he wrote to her. "I am sure it must be a matter of great comfort and pleasure to you to have this little place of your own at Madison. You have taken such a deep interest in the work there and now you will feel more than ever that you are a part of it. I know Dr. Sutherland appreciates so much having you there. He has often mentioned it to me."[25]

The Final Showdown

The Year 1921
(The collection contains no 1920 letters)

"Dear Sister Scott:--" Dr. Magan wrote on February 17, 1921, "I find that I will not be able to get to Madison as soon as I had expected. As it stands now, I will be there about the middle of March."[1]

He needed much support from his Tennessee friends that year. Political problems once again interfered with the College of Medical Evangelists attaining a Grade A rating. Back in 1919, the board pressed him to finish the needed buildings to satisfy the American Medical Association requirements. Now, his superiors had resumed their stalling.

"The General Conference brethren are making things very hard for us here," he wrote to Mrs. Scott. "The Lord has always thwarted their designs against the school in days gone by, and I have all confidence that He will thwart them again, but just at present on account of the Musgrave report, and their attitude to it, we are passing through the deepest kind of waters."[2] The College of Medical Evangelists was not quite ready for full recognition. An American Medical Association evaluation called for some changes that the top General Conference officers on the Board of Directors didn't want to make. The future of the medical school with its tenuous B rating was once again in doubt. "I am enclosing copy of a letter I have just received from Dr. Kretchmar in London, and also copy of my reply, which I thought you would like to have," he continued. "I will also enclose copy of a letter I have written to Dr. Amyes in Edinborough, [Edinburgh] which will give you a little bit of an idea about the troubles we are having with the General Conference. They are doing their best to limit our attendance, and some of them at least are conducting a campaign which if it was not for the good hand of God watching over us, might prove disastrous. I want to have a long conference with you all when I get to Madison. I don't suppose these men intend to be mean, but they are doing everything in their power to shut down on us. They have always howled around and talked about the immense amount of money it was costing to run the medical college, but we have done so well in every Department this past year that we are able to run the coming year without one cent of help from them—that is, as far as operating expenses are concerned. But they will not give us one cent for buildings or anything else. We are going to raise all the money, however, for our new building out here on the Coast, and are commencing work on it today. But we are going to be in bad shape for a nurses dormitory. I am going to make the plea of my life at the Spring Council in Washington for help on that, but I have my doubts about getting it. The only dormitory we have ever had is the building which you so kindly gave us when we first started. That holds 32 people. We now have something like 80 nurses, which means that more than half of them will be scattered all over this end of town, and this says nothing about the girls in the medical classes and our faithful bookkeepers, stenographers and social service workers. In a way it gets to be tiresome—trying to run an institution for men who at heart don't want it, and if it were not that I believe the good Lord wants it and that His hand is over all, and that I love the dear lads here who are coming to this school at far greater expense than they would be at in any of these worldly schools in order that they may imbibe the principles of this Message, I would be tempted to leave the whole thing and go at it from an independent standpoint where I would not eternally have this handicap. However, I suppose it is good for us or the Lord would not let it be. Please keep all of this confidential."[3] Before the report became public, he sent an advance copy of it to Mrs. Scott.

"I am enclosing in this a very confidential document for Professor Sutherland, Mrs. Druillard, Miss DeGraw[4] and yourself to read," he wrote. "Kindly return it to me when you are finished, and please do not permit any copies of the same to be made. I refer to the report of Dr. W. A. Musgrave, Mr. Cellestine, J. Sullivan and Mr. Hartley Peart on this medical college which they have made to the Council on Medical Education and Hospitals of the American Medical Association. This report to you folks will be, I am sure, most interesting, illuminating and enlightening, but please keep it to yourselves and do not give it any circulation whatsoever. My reason for asking this is that the document which I am sending you is a copy of the report as they sent it to the Council on Medical Education in Chicago. I have received this because I am a member of the committee which examined us, namely, the American Medical Association Committee on Medical Education and Hospitals in the State of California, but of course I did not sit or act with the Committee in our own case at all, and had no conversation with them in regard to their findings whatsoever. Dr. Musgrave will shortly furnish a report for our Board of Trustees and Faculty which will embody the things written in this report, but which will put the findings and recommendations in more formal style and setting for the perusal of said Trustees and faculty. I will not comment upon this report at any length, but I think it shows how slow we are to learn and to gain and hold the opportunities which we might have. Sometimes I feel most disheartened when I think of all the hard toil we have put in here, to build up something worthy of God's name in the earth, and then to have our rating held up because of certain denominational policies which we are powerless to amend or abrogate."[5] The Musgrave Report disapproved of the chief executive officer of the board serving as school business manager, giving him administrative authority over the president and the dean. Other recommendations were to make the Los Angeles campus the school headquarters, enlarge the medical library, increase the teaching personnel, raise the budget by 25 percent, and appoint an executive committee from the board with broad administrative powers.[6]

This report posed a new challenge to the religious faith of Dr. Magan and his supporters.

The real problem seemed to be apathy to Adventist medical work within the highest levels of the General Conference administration.

"I thank you for returning the report to me which I sent you in confidence," Magan wrote to Mrs. Scott regarding the Musgrave Report. "Since then we have had a long discussion with Elders Daniells and Knox. At first they were very much inclined to attribute the entire report to your humble servant. This was so ridiculous however, that it could not possibly stick, but it was very hard for them to get it out of their heads that I had not a great deal to do with inspiring it. We had a pretty strenuous time together for a while—Dr. Thomason, Dr. Evans and myself on one side; Elders Daniells, Knox and Mr. Bowen on the other. It reminded me of some of the meetings which Dr. Sutherland and I used to have with Elder Daniells in the early years of this century over the whole medical question; and also a bit later on when we first went to Tennessee. At first these men were not inclined to do anything at all looking toward meeting the requirements of the American Medical Association. However, their position in this was soon made to appear so utterly untenable that they are willing now to sit down quietly with us somewhere along the first of the year and discuss the whole matter. I feel that it will take an immense amount of the great and good wisdom of the good God to get by with them as far as the school is concerned. As far as I am concerned, from one standpoint I care but little. I have worked like a slave ever since I have been here, and my sole desire, as far as the school is concerned, is to put it where the Lord would have it, and to make it the light in the earth He designs it shall be. We have been told in the Spirit of Prophecy that we must work in harmony with 'the legal requirements of the State and nation in the matter of training our young physicians.' It seems very difficult for these men to get this matter clear in their minds. I am sure Doctor Sutherland, however, can help explain this to you. They do not see what business the American Medical Association has to dictate to us concerning medical education. They want to run everything their own way from Washington just as they please, and this, as I understand it, the Council on Medical Education will not tolerate. One thing certain—if they refuse to do the thing which the Council on Medical Education and Hospitals of the American Medical Association request them to do, the school will be closed, for the American Medical Association will simply shove it down into the 'C' grade—then these brethren will be in a place where they will have to explain to the people that they have caused the closing of the school because of their determination not to allow the physicians to have anything to say to the financial management; not to permit the headquarters of the school to be in Los Angeles, and not to agree to having an executive committee with reasonable powers. They are going to be in a mighty hard place when they go up against this proposition, because Seventh-day Adventists do have executive committees, and many of our college presidents are also the business managers of the institutions over which they preside, and I don't believe that these leading brethren will ever be able to face the storm of criticism that they will be bound to meet if they force a situation which will mean the closing of the school."[7]

Sutherland and Magan had never been able to agree with the legendary A. G. Daniells on how to conduct Adventist medical work. They wanted to start a sanitarium in Berrien Springs, Michigan, after the Battle Creek Sanitarium burned down. The failure of that idea had been one reason they left Michigan for Tennessee. Little had changed during the twenty years since then.

E. A. Sutherland summed up the problem in a letter to Dr. Magan.

"I know you brethren will not be able to do very much over the A.M.A. report except to swallow it," he wrote to Magan regarding the Musgrave Report. "I appreciate that it is a pill of much bitterness, but they have had many warnings, and they must learn to see the medical side of the

Third Angels Message. They have never seen anything much except the evangelistic side, and I hope you will 'stand pat' on the matter, for they certainly must begin to realize that if they are going to do medical work in the world, they have got to recognize at least the world's viewpoint. This does not mean apostasy or compromise, but it means to look at things at least as the other fellow looks at them, which is very hard for many of the brethren to do. They have been so inclined to feel the authority of position rather than ability that it will be hard for them to come across."[8]

Arthur Grosvenor Daniells had caught the spirit of the Advent pioneers and, during twenty breathtaking years as president of the General Conference, taken Adventism into the big leagues with a growing number of overseas missionaries, publishing houses, colleges, and an impressive church conference structure at all levels; but great organizer that he was, he left physicians out of his grand program.

For example, as the general approach to North America, the 1905 General Conference session, "realizing that multitudes are 'in the valley of decision,' and that the time has fully come when the Master pleads with every child of his to 'go out quickly into the streets and lanes of the city' and 'into the highways and hedges' to bid the hungry and perishing to the marriage feast," recommended the following "great missionary campaign for the promulgation of the third angel's message."

1. A *Review & Herald* subscription in every Sabbath-keeping home.
2. A church-wide campaign to increase the circulation of missionary periodicals.
3. Encouraging members in the sale of Adventist books.
4. Developing evangelical interest by the liberal use of tracts, giving Bible studies in individuals' homes, and missionary correspondence.[9]

Later in the same year, Elder Daniells defined his role in the evolving organization of the church, again not including medical missionary work in his goals.

He wrote in the *Review*. "Should it be asked what the president will do with so many details assigned to others, I will state that he hopes to be able to give some attention to many important, weighty interests of a general character which he has seriously neglected in order to attend to more local details. The great problems of our mission fields, the translation, production, and distribution of literature in behalf of the great masses of humanity now in darkness of heathenism, the improvement and enlargement of our ministry, the development of our educational work, and the visiting of distant mission fields to assist in organizing and strengthening the work begun are some of the interests which the president of the General Conference may now be able to give proper attention. They are worthy of the best service he is able to render."[10]

Giving medical work low priority—or no role at all--apparently pervaded all levels of Adventist church administration.

"There seems to be a determined campaign on all over the country to prevent students from coming here," Magan shared with Mrs. Scott. "Every place I go I find myself confronted with statements that, the President of our Union, or the President of our Conference has warned us not to study medicine—that all our young doctors apostatize—that the denomination does not need Doctors and medical workers, but preachers. One young man who recently filled out his questionnaire for me, answering the question as to what experiences he had passed through in order to come to medical college, stated that when he was at Berrien Springs the president of the school had constantly warned him against coming here— that when Elder Shaw had visited the school he had talked with him a couple of hours endeavoring to persuade him from his purpose of taking the medical course—that his visit was followed in a few months by Elder Kern who had a similar mission, and that then Elder Wiest had made a special trip to see his father and to beg his father not to let him study medicine. You can imagine something of the feeling these young men have toward our ministry when this is the kind of a send off that they get to medical school; and this is not an isolated case. I could tell you of dozens of others just as pronounced as this."[11]

Dr. Magan's faith was still strong.

"What the end will be I do not know beyond that I am certain that a kind Father in Heaven is determined in spite of all the workings of Satan and the misunderstandings of men, to have a medical work of his own in the world that will be a credit to Him when he comes. And in the meantime we must labor on patiently and perseveringly until we can get on to better ground than we are now."[12]

Some Adventist leaders did not take health reform seriously, according to one report.

"On the blanks which we require to be filled out there are a number of questions relative to the standing of the student on health questions," Dr. Magan wrote to Mrs. Scott in another letter. "Professor Smith, the president of the College, told me frankly and candidly 'There is no health question in the North Pacific Union Conference. I never hear the subject discussed. All of our teachers, as well as the students, eat flesh foods. Our ministers all do it and I supposed that abstaining from flesh foods was no longer a tenant [tenet] of the Seventh-day Adventist faith.' This is typical of the state of affairs I think generally, throughout our conferences. A few days after my talk with President Smith I was in Portland, Oregon, in a restaurant with Dr. Holden, the Business Manager of the Portland Sanitarium, and two of the very most prominent General Conference ministers. The restaurant was a kind of a semi-cafeteria place where you can get anything in the world that you wanted to eat. You can imagine my surprise when the business manager of the Portland Sanitarium ordered a beef steak as high as a bicycle saddle and when one of the General Conference ministers, with whom you are very well acquainted, ordered a salmon steak of similar proportions, and openly stated that he did not feel in doing so he was in any way transgressing our health principles. This looks to me that if a certain prophet of ancient times were alive again . . . a little something more to say than blindness in part hath come upon Israel."[13]

"Elder Daniells has talked to me a good deal... about becoming General Conference Medical Secretary, but I see no light in anything of that kind, for the present, at any rate. Especially, as long as he and his fellows take the attitude toward us that they do. I believe Elder Daniells honestly wants medical missionary work done, but he has not got it straight in his head that loyalty to the health principles as laid down in the Spirit of Prophecy is the vital fundamental thing in all our medical missionary work, and as long as he is determined to leave this out, things are going to go hard or our training is going to come from another quarter."[14]

Dr. Magan's disagreements with Elder Daniells seemed to come as no surprise to Mrs. Scott.

"I was interested in all you wrote about your troubles with the brethren and the rating of the school," she replied. "I understand that Elder Daniells suggests that they omit the expense of a General Conference this year. Would that mean there would be no election?"[15]

"I wonder how it will be settled about the pleasing of the A.M.A. and the Council on Medical Education," she wrote again. "I cannot think that that school has completed its work yet. But the Lord may want us to get a higher standard in some things, regarding the dispensation of drugs and so on, and will allow us to get shaken up that we may wake up to the supreme importance of coming up to His standard in moral things."[16]

"As far as getting things settled between the brethren and the A.M.A.—they will all get settled in God's good time," Dr. Magan replied. "The brethren dare not do otherwise. The Lord is certainly blessing the school. If He were not, He would not be sending us the tremendous numbers of students which He is sending, and our graduates would not be having the great experiences they are having in their work. We are also doing a tremendous amount of work—taking these young preachers and their wives whom the General Conference sends to foreign fields, and giving them short courses from three to six months here. This has become a great feature of our work, and it is accomplishing much."[17]

The good news was that attempts to discourage students from entering medical school there were apparently not working.

"I feel very, very sorry that it was impossible for you to come out here with your girls when they came this fall," Dr. Magan wrote. "This morning we had our first Assembly' in the chapel. I have never looked on such a magnificent company of students in my life, and I have never known the school to open with such a splendid spiritual atmosphere as it opens with this year. I am trying to shift a lot of my routine duties so that I can give more time to the spiritual work of the school. We have been under a great strain here endeavoring to keep alive during the war, getting up our buildings, struggling against tremendous odds with the American Medical Association, etc. You may remember my having told you once a sentence which Sister White wrote in regard to the founding of our medical college; namely, that 'it pleased the Lord that our medical college should come into being at a time when the rivers of difficulty were full and overflowing their banks.' There has been one struggle after another here, and all of the rivers of difficulty have not subsided from the high water mark yet by any means.[18]

"We have an immense number of applications for the first year medical class, for this fall, so much so that we are at our wits end to know what to do with them. We have already taken in about 70, and I think altogether have had considerably over 100 applications. However, some of these were not the proper kind of students to take and others had not completed their pre-medical work, so on the whole, I think we are going to be able to care for all of those who should be taken care of. But it is a serious proposition, and a big undertaking. We do not begin to have even the humblest cottages to put all of these students in, and the housing problem is a very, very serious one with us."[19]

The school year itself seemed to end fine.

"We had our graduating exercises Saturday night at Loma Linda and had really a very nice time," he wrote. "I have never seen a graduating class more simply dressed than was this one. There were no ribbons or bouquets and the girls wore the simplest kind of black dresses. We had only a few simple flowers for decoration in the chapel. Dr. George Harding [younger brother of President Warren Harding] gave the address. It was very, very good and well received by all. Even the preachers were highly delighted with it, although they had previously scolded me for having him give the address due to the fact that he is not in the 'regular channel.' The boys are all very busy now with getting ready for the State Board which comes the end of June."[20]

The term "regular channel" seemed to imply people employed within the official conference structure. He applied it to Mrs. Scott when remarking, in this same letter, that "I laughed at your quoted remark relative to the 'regular channel.' I am glad to know that you are so orthodox. The brethren ought to love you more dearly than they do on[21] account of this good trait in your character."

Dr. Magan wrote of some fine quality people joining him there. "We have word that the Brownsbergers [from Fletcher, North Carolina] are on the way, and that they will be with us a little before school opens. We will all be glad to see them, and will do our best to make things happy for them when they come. It will not be very long until Miss Noble, Miss Dale, and later the Brownsbergers and Lew Wallace will be ready to go back south, and then you will have a contingent for work in that part of the world. I am very, very thankful for this."[22]

Later on he wrote, "The Brownsbergers have arrived here all safe, and seem exceedingly happy. I have had several good talks with them when I have been out at Loma Linda. Miss Marguerite Coffin is also here. I think she has about decided that it will be best for her to take the regular nurses' course. Since she intends to become the wife of a man who expects to be a doctor, she will I am sure do better in fitting herself along the nursing line so that she can work with her husband. As I understand it, she is a good teacher already."[23]

Representatives from prominent Adventist families were there, such as Hester Kellogg, sister of Dr. John Harvey Kellogg, and her daughter Gertrude. "Gertrude is sick and the mother far from well."[24] Highland Butler, son of former General Conference President George I. Butler, had rejoined Adventism after being out for eighteen years, married an Adventist woman of means, and showed possibilities of starting a rural extension of the White Memorial Hospital a few miles out of town.[25] He and Dr. George Hare, brother-in-law of Arthur G. Daniells, had founded a successful company of Seventh-day Adventist self-supporting workers near Fresno, California.[26] Grosvenor Daniells, son of Arthur G. Daniells, had enrolled at Loma Linda. "I think he is trying to do what is right," commented Dr. Magan.[27]

Some former students were doing well. "You will be interested to know that Dr. Earle J. Gardner and Dr. Arthur Kretchmar have passed their final examinations in London on Obstetrics, Gynecology, Medicine, Pediatrics and Dermatology. There were 63 up for the examination, and 11 passed. Both of them received honors, and were highly complimented by the Board, being told that they were 'an honor to their school and their country.' We all feel very happy over this. To get by when so many perished is a great thing, and to pass on the first trial is if anything a still greater thing. They now have everything off except surgery, which they will take in October. We are all of good hope and courage that they will get by then."[28]

The best news he had for her was that some graduates of the College of Medical Evangelists would soon head back to the South.

"I am sure that when all of these young folks—Miss Noble, the Brownsbergers, Lew Wallace, Marguerite Coffin and Miss Dale have finished their training, you will have a great company for the work in the South. There is no question in my mind that when that day is reached, the work of Madison can go forward by leaps and bounds."[29]

"I am glad for the good report you have given of the Madison group whose hearts Loma Linda has stolen for the present," Mrs. Scott wrote to Magan. "They are all enjoying their work, they tell us, but it is good to hear what you say about them."[30]

Another letter said the same thing.

"I hear from Marguerite quite often and from Blanche and Elsie occasionally and some of the other girls. They seem to be enjoying their work there very much. We can hardly wait until they get through and come back again. They always enjoy your visits and talks."[31]

Dr. Magan always did all he could to furnish desperately needed physicians and other medical workers to his fellow workers in the underprivileged South. Dr. Lew Wallace was one of the leading physicians at Madison Hospital for many years. The Brownsberger family was prominent at the Fletcher unit of Madison in North Carolina.

Mrs. Scott also continued financially supporting Mary Dale and Ethel Hennessy, and helped other young women as well. "One thing is certain,"

Dr. Magan wrote to her. "The South is going to get the bulk of the very best of our young women students. This is due to you, who is [sic] putting money into them. The General Conference does not seem inclined to invest a cent in these girls."[32]

His appeal at the Spring Council apparently paid off, for the General Conference officers had contributed enough money for a needed dormitory.

"We are building our new nurses' home here. I succeeded in getting the General Conference to put up the money for it—or at least put up $40,000. It will house approximately 82 young women besides giving us a dining room and serving room for the entire school family, medical evangelists and nurses. It also will contain two classrooms for the nurses. I had a big time to get this but finally got it. I think the brethren generally were afraid of the consequences that might follow if they did not give it to us: it is quite an undertaking to look after the moral and spiritual welfare of so many young men and women in this great city. I am deeply thankful to God that thus far nothing unfortunate has happened, and on the whole we have gotten along very well."[33]

Then his roller coaster ride with A.G. Daniells took another turn.

"Elder Daniells has gotten a notion into his head of late that he wants to make me medical secretary for the General Conference with headquarters in Washington. I know I do not have much sense, but I think I still have a sufficient number of gray cells yet to keep me out of any such a move as this. The Elder is honest enough and means well, but that thing, to my mind, is about as near a political death as the vice presidency of the United States. I do feel that there is a great need for someone to give his time in large part at least to getting these young fellows that we graduate connected with the work. In other words, someone has got to plan work for them—to organize medical missionary units for the stricken countries of Europe, etc., but if they will give me more time and help I can do that just as well from here as from Washington. In other words, it looks to me we will be able to accomplish a great deal more by sticking together here for a while than by separating. However, I am very glad that Elder Daniells has gotten hold of the idea that it is now the day and generation to do something for the medical work, and to push it. This means a great deal."[34]

False rumors were a problem.

"I can not help but feel that someone is giving you altogether erroneous information about the dispensation of drugs here," Dr. Magan wrote.

"You have referred to it several times in your letters of late. We hear just the same things here about Madison, but I don't believe a word of it. It was reported to me the other day by someone who had been there that Dr. Sutherland just stuffed his patients with drugs. I have no more idea that that is true than I have that you are a Methodist or a Mormon—or saying mass at six o'clock in the morning. As I wrote you in a previous letter, it is impossible to give hydrotherapy to an average of 225 patients a day, who after they paid a dime entry fee to the Dispensary are paying everything they can—and these few dimes are all we have on which to run the Dispensary. I am doing my best now to get our dietetic business on a better basis. After that, I want to go after more money for hydrotherapy, physiotherapy, electrotherapy and massage and Swedish movement equipment."[35]

Then came evidence of the strain under which Magan had been laboring.

"I know you think I am a great heathen and very bad, but I am doing the very best I can."[36]

He need not have worried.

"My dear Doctor Magan," she replied, "your two letters of October 20 and 24 respectively are at hand. First of all, I want to assure you that I have confidence in your efforts to bring the College up to the highest standard set by the Testimonies. I know that is your aim, and that you are striving against great odds. The Lord has helped you to do wonderful things for that institution, and a great deal of good has been accomplished for humanity. Do not get the idea that I doubt that. But as you say, the diet phase needs greater emphasis which can be done by putting it on a better basis; and the simple methods (we call them simple) which the Lord has instructed us to use are to be more and more brought to the front. I have confidence that you are doing all you can to do this. If you were the only one who wanted it done, with God you would be the majority. But of course it takes time. I think the movement you have on foot for having the students study these various points from the Testimonies will be a wonderful help. I am glad Mary Dale takes such an interest in this."[37]

Troubles of her own forced a temporary cutback in giving.

"Now, don't imagine that I am hesitating for fear the institution may not be coming up on all these things, in regard to the donation I promised if I received the dividend. I have simply been waiting for that dividend ever since. It looks as if I am not going to get it at all, and that you had better not count on it. I am very sorry, but you will remember that when you were here I mentioned the possibility of no dividend being declared. So this ties my hands."³⁸

She was still deeply interested and involved in the financial affairs of the school, as the following letter shows.

"Now Sister Scott, I want to ask you to do something to help me out in an emergency," he wrote to her in November. "It is this: you have already given us $3,900 in cash on the Dietetic - #3 Hospital unit, and a mortgage for $3,000. The mortgage I have not sold yet, as there were some technical things wrong with the papers that Mr. Tymen Owens of Kemper B. Campbell's office is fixing up. He will send these to you, and as soon as I get them back, I am sure I can without difficulty dispose of the mortgage, which will make us, including the money covered by the receipt which I am including in this, $6,090 on the #3 Dietetic unit, plus some interest that will be accruing to this account on the $3,000 which has been lying here in the bank for some time. The bank is paying us four per cent on this.

"Now, my trouble is this: the obstetrical unit and the private room pavilion unit are finished all but the linoleum for the floors, beds, mattresses, furniture and linen. I judge that these items will cost probably in the neighborhood of seven or eight thousand dollars. I have plenty of good pledges to cover them, but on account of the price of cotton, barley and wheat I am held up on collecting for a lot of these pledges. They are from good men like Brother Nis Hansen, whom I think you know, and whom Brother Sutherland knows very, very well. But as above stated, they will be a bit slow coming in. Now I want your permission to temporarily use the money I have from you so that I can get the furniture and get into these buildings—so that a number of these poor women in this town will not be deprived of proper care in childbirth. On account of the financial situation in the West at present there is terrible suffering amongst the poor here now, and it seems too bad to let these buildings lie idle until we can get these pledges in. I will promise you to get the money and replace this within a reasonable time, so we can go ahead on the third unit. If this is satisfactory to you, please write me immediately. I have already gotten money enough to finish up the girls' dormitory, and we will move them into that now in two or three weeks."³⁹

A shift in the economy had caused a brief financial recession in 1920-21.

"It is just possible I may see you all at Madison pretty soon. I have a lead from one of 'the merchant princes of the earth' that may mean quite a bit of money to help out on this Dietetic unit that you have so nobly started for us. This may take me to New York City."[40]

Then, as 1921 ended, the political climate at the College of Medical Evangelists seemed headed for change.

"I am praying much," Dr. Magan wrote to Mrs. Scott in a confidential letter. "It looks to me that we are on the eve of a tremendous upheaval in our work. I have never thought this until recently, but I am certain we are facing something now. I will tell you a tale, and this, as well as this whole letter, for all of you at Madison, but please keep it confidential and on no account quote me.

"As I understand it, the General Conference Council, just held in Minneapolis, was a rutty, rocky affair. It would appear that clouds have been gathering against the inner cabinet of the denomination at Washington for some time. A large number of the near-leaders have been becoming more and more opposed to Daniells, Knox, Kern, Charles Thompson and Company. At the Spring Council trouble began to brew. On the way to Minneapolis this fall I understand a large number of these men first at Berrien Springs and then in Chicago held several meetings where they discussed what should happen at the next General Conference. One thing seemed to be settled, that when a man has been holding the office of President of the General Conference for over 20 years he has held it plenty long enough. This seems to be their slogan but they have a large number of other grievances of interference in their work, arbitrary measures, etc.

"When these men reached Minneapolis, they openly held meetings by themselves, but to which Daniells and Knox were not invited, and further discussed what they would do and what they would not do in the matter of the coming elections in San Francisco. Of course, word of all this soon reached the President and Treasurer of the General Conference. They finally called a meeting and held the same behind closed doors. No one was permitted to attend except members of the General Conference Committee. At this meeting Daniells made a speech. He began by stating that he wanted to discuss three propositions. First, familiarity between denominational officials and their women stenographers and helpers; second, criticism of leading men; third, politics in regard to the elections at the next General Conference. I am told that everybody knew that numbers 1 and 2 were simply starters to get at the real thing that was on his mind. He talked at length on the wickedness of criticizing leading men and told how in older days this was not tolerated, but how now more novices in the work felt free to pick their leaders to pieces in the most irreligious fashion. Finally, he got down to the main subject. He reviewed the course of those preachers in holding meetings at which they discussed what they were going to do with him at the next General Conference, and told how wicked this was. Then he proceeded to relate how he and Knox had gone off into the woods somewhere together and spent a day discussing things. At the end of the day both decided that under no consideration would either of them run for office at the next General Conference. But he further related that the next day, or some time later, new light had come to him to the end that he had done wrong in deciding he would not run again, and that he had made up his mind if it should appear to be the Lord's will that he become president of the General Conference again that he would take the position. He stated that Knox stood pat on the proposition they had agreed upon and would not under any circumstances be Treasurer again of the General Conference. As I understand it, his speech was received with silence. There was no response and the assembled host filed out quietly at the close of it.

"The next day, nothing was said, but the day after bedlam broke loose and men began to assert their rights, understand that the old Chief felt very badly and that he told a number of his friends he was completely disheartened and that he did not preside at more than half the meetings of the Minneapolis Council. I understand that a large number of Union Conference presidents and Union workers [felt] that his interference in the John Christian case in this Union was most unwarranted and they are openly planning to fix him for it.

"Now this whole thing is inexpressibly sad. I wish very much that you and Dr. Sutherland could be at San Francisco. It is going to be an epic-making Conference, I am sure, and changes are bound to come."[41]

"Elder Daniells and Elder Knox have been bound and determined to bind the Medical College about with strong cords," he continued. "God is not in the thing and their program is doomed to failure. I am as certain of this as I am that I breathe. Their whole course at the present time is akin to the course they took in the early days when Sister White was trying to found this work. I have no confidence that God is with them in their determination to set up a one-man, kingly power in the Medical College. Dr. Sutherland can tell you all about the story of this program during the days of Irwin when he and I put Daniells into the presidency in 1901. I believe Elder Daniells is a godly man and means well, and from very many standpoints he has done a great work, but I am certain that that time has arrived when God is going to order a change in affairs."[42]

Loma Linda Marches On

Post-1921 Letters

No letters between Lida Scott and Percy Magan are on the file for the year 1922. Two major events affected the College of Medical Evangelists that year.

The General Conference session of 1922 ended the twenty-year tenure of Arthur G. Daniells as president and elected William A. Spicer to replace him. The same delegates chose W. T. Knox to be a general field secretary and replaced him as treasurer with J. L. Shaw.[1]

The board voted in the spring of 1922 to carry out the Musgrave recommendations for reorganization. The constituency affirmed this action, and on November 16, 1922, the College of Medical Evangelists finally received the official Grade A rating.[2]

"Certainly you are to be congratulated that you have obtained the A grade at last for your school," wrote Dr. John Harvey Kellogg to Dr. Magan. "Providence has seemed to favor your schemes, especially in the working out of the Southern California Medical School and by giving you an opportunity to demand recognition which you otherwise might not have gotten."[3]

Dr. Kellogg then made a classic statement expressing the purpose of Adventist medical missionary work. "Now if you will only raise your standard so as to make sure that the men and women who go out from your school are real missionaries and not merely commercial doctors, you may accomplish something really worthwhile, but if you run a medical school which is not radically different from other medical schools in the country, it will not be worthwhile. I think you ought to make your students feel that it is a criminal thing for them to use the advantages which have been secured through the self-sacrificing of hundreds of honest men and women merely to prepare themselves for a money-getting vocation. Such a course looks to me like down right thievery. Every one of your students ought to go out as an apostle of health reform and medical reform. It is not worthwhile to bother with any others."[4] Some of the letters following accreditation concerned an "industrial" plan of education.

"I was so glad to get your excellent letter of January 9," Dr. Magan wrote to Mrs. Scott early in 1923. "It has been a long time since I have heard from you. I am glad you enjoyed what we wrote relative to the 'A Grade' rating for the medical school.

"We are now turning our attention very forcibly to the matter of the industrial plan of work for our students," he continued. "The Freshman class at Loma Linda are very strongly in favor of it. The Sophomore class not so much. I think there is a general good feeling about it here at Los Angeles, but of course it will never affect these two classes, as one of them will graduate in May, and the others will be Seniors next year and we hardly feel that we can start it for each class at once."[5]

In this same letter, he seemed grateful to have Mrs. Scott as a financial supporter because one of his other backers had fallen on hard times.

"Yesterday we held a Board meeting practically devoted to this question. Our mutual friend, Glenn Calkins, whom you met at Long Beach, was with us. He is very deeply interested, and I believe will see his way clear to join us in the business end of the new Department, but the poor man is having his troubles. He stands in a good way to lose all that he has. This, for a new Adventist who is really devoted, and had wanted to use his money in the Cause, is a serious blow. The oil wells on Signal Hill, Long Beach are going dry. He was very deep in the oil prospect and had borrowed an immense amount of money to get into it. Now, this money will have to be paid back from his other interests, as the wells are failing up on production. Then he has speculated in wheat for a number of years, and his deals this year have gone against him heavily."[6]

With accreditation behind him, Magan started becoming philosophical about the misrepresentations.

"In addition to all of this a number of that class of people whom the Bible tells us to love; namely, our enemies, have been telling him [Calkins] what frightful sinners we all are in the Medical College. I think, however, we got him pretty well straightened out on this, but no stone has been left unturned by these friends in their endeavor to prevent him [from] joining us. I think a good letter from you would be of interest to him, and I would appreciate it if you would write him. Do not go into the details of how he is losing his money on that side of it—just mention that you understand that financial matters have become much more difficult for him than he had expected."[7]

Magan implied that his enemies had helped more than hurt him.

"I do not know what attitude the brethren are going to take about the matter. I learned that one of those whom I am instructed to love, has been telling that I was endeavoring to inject a lot of my crazy Madison notions into the Medical School. It is rather amusing, as Dr. Evans feels that this is his pet scheme—that I have been very slow in helping him to push it. However, my lover will probably live through the thing, and I will too. You know, Sister Scott, there is a real philosophy in those words of the Master, 'Love your enemies.' Our enemies are really better friends to us than our friends, for they are not at all afraid to tell us or to tell other people our sins, failures and mistakes; and when they tell other people of course it nearly always gets around to us so we get the benefit anyway. As a matter of fact our enemies accomplish a great deal more good for us in our lives than our friends."[8]

He then explained how the enemies of Joseph and Mordecai in Old Testament times had wound up elevating them.

"You certainly look at it in the right way and get a blessing where many would get a spoiled disposition," replied Mrs. Scott. "You give me a new idea as to the way we should look at these would-be enemies who are our best friends. My father used to say, 'Court criticism. Your enemies will tell you more than you ought to know about yourself than you will ever get from your friends.'"[9]

Another letter showed the give-and-take relationship of Percy Magan with his Madison supporters.

For his part, he had always done all he could to send them needed medical professionals and now had something to offer. Some CME graduates would intern at Protestant Hospital in Nashville, Tennessee, later known as Baptist Hospital.

"I am sending you herewith copy of letter I have written Van Sanders regarding the boys who are going to intern at the Protestant next year, and also about Dr. Cleo Chastain," he wrote to Dr. Sutherland and Mrs. Scott early in 1926. "I have had a long talk with her since you left, and she is willing to work on the program that you and I outlined for her provided the same can be put into force. I believe this will be a fine thing to do.

"I never can tell you how much we all enjoyed your visit here," he continued, "and I never will be able to express my appreciation for all that Mrs. Scott has done in our trials and difficulties at this place. I feel more thankful than I can tell that these three young men are going to the Protestant, and that Doctor Chastain will go provided matters can be arranged for her. Doctor Brunie seems to be very happy and thoroughly alive to the idea of going and to the needs of the South. Yolanda [daughter of E. A. Sutherland] seems to dove-tail into his program very nicely."[10]

Although Magan was sending them doctors, he still needed money for the medical school.

"Now, I am wondering if you two folks could do something to interest Mrs. Druillard and Mrs. Gotzian in helping us on our new physiotherapy building," he continued. "I will have to raise all told somewhere in the neighborhood of $60,000, and I have to raise it amongst old friends, and am not allowed to do anything through the regular channels, which of course makes my path doubly hard. The Lord has wonderfully blessed in bringing us means so far. Mr. Amos Prescott, who as you know is not an Adventist, has already paid in $10,000, and Mrs. Scott's gift of $3,000 will be available within a very short time, as I understand it. Mrs. Covington gave me $500 and I have $600 from Dr. George Harding, and a few other small pledges.

Now I thought, if possible, Mrs. Gotzian and Mrs. Druillard might be interested to give us at least $1,000 each, especially in view of the great need and the purpose for which the money is desired. Both of these women, I know, have always felt that we used too many drugs here. I think it is true that we do, but we have been in a hard place as we have had no building or equipment with which to carry on rational treatment. When we first came here the thing we had to do was to get a bit of land. Our land alone in this city cost more than double the price paid originally for our farm in Madison.... The next thing that had to be was some space for beds and a kitchen, and a few class rooms, and dormitory for our nurses. It has taken years and a lot of money to build up even this. But I feel that the time has come when we must roll away the reproach over this drug question and get us a good large building where we can carry on this work in a way that will be pleasing to the Lord. We will have to get this money from people who are interested in the real health reform principles of this message, and you know their numbers are not legion. How I will greatly appreciate it if you will do all you legitimately can with Mrs. Druillard and Mrs. Gotzian to get some help for us. I am writing them today and am enclosing copy of my letter.

"I hate to be such a bother to you, but I trust that in other ways we may be able to do something to compensate."[11]

According to a letter from Magan in June 1926, Lida Scott donated $5,000 to the Physiotherapy Building in the preceding March. In response to her request, he listed all the financial gifts that Mrs. Scott had made to

Loma Linda starting in 1913. At that point, it amounted to $28,104.90, not counting the financial aid to students and the $30,000 diversionary gift from Madison College to start the White Memorial Hospital.[12] In 1917, $5,000 was equivalent to $100,000 in today's economy.

Magan also signed an agreement to help raise $10,000 for his Madison friends in exchange for a gift of that amount to start a new unit of the White Memorial Hospital. He would try to do this within three years after he received the $10,000 because he knew they needed the money for their own enterprises in the South.[13]

"Dear Folks," Dr. Magan wrote to Dr. Sutherland and Mrs. Scott on March 3, 1929, also sending a copy of the letter to May Covington, a donor in Minden, Nebraska, "I am afraid that I have made you good folks a world of trouble over the matter of the $10,000 for the new building at the White Memorial, but I never can tell Mrs. Scott how very, very deeply I appreciate all of her kindness to us in the matter of money and of support in a thousand different ways. Over and over again I have said, and have told many others, that when the books of God are opened in the Judgment the credit of bringing the medical school to its birth and of keeping it alive will belong to three women—Lida F. Scott, May Covington and Josephine Gotzian. The rest of us have in a way merely been instruments in the hands of this trinity. Had it not been for the tremendous support given us by Mrs. Gotzian when we first started there would not have been any Loma Linda. Then came the hard, hard days of 1915 when the General Conference brethren were of a mind to either close the school altogether or restrict it to two years of work, which in the end would have been just the same thing. It was at this juncture that Mrs. Gotzian again came forward with, as I recollect it, some $15,000.

"Mrs. Scott stood by and made us a gift of Montclair Cottage, the first home we had for our nurses, which was built as I recollect it at a cost of somewhere in the neighborhood of $8,000," he continued. "Then came our struggle to get up what is now known as the service building,-- kitchens, laboratories, classrooms, laboratory, and the cafeteria for our help to eat in. Mrs. Scott was far and away the largest contributor to this building. I will never forget her kindly willingness, and more than willingness in the city of Chicago. You and I, Ed, talked with her there at the Great Northern Hotel, and Mrs. Scott practically drained her accounts in every bank where she had money in order to give us $6,000 without delay."[14]

Magan's Nebraska friends also supported him at this critical time.

"Miss Covington gave Minden Cottage, which was a matter of another $8,000, and her dear old mother Covington Cottage," he noted. "Since then of course Mrs. Scott has come to our rescue a number of times. Always so kindly even when she felt that she wanted to put money elsewhere. At times I have felt that both of you must have [been] terribly disappointed the way a number of those whom Mrs. Scott and others have helped through school for the sake of the work at Madison have turned out. The failure of Julian Gant to connect with Madison after all that was done for him is heartbreaking. The experience with little Yolanda, whom I dearly love, I know has been a great trial to you both. Mr. Mazie Palleson I suppose is another case of the same kind. What to do about these things I know not. They are heart rending. The only comfort I see in your part of it is that you are not the only ones who get it this way. We get it just exactly the same here in the medical school, and Ed, I think you have told me many, many times that you have it with your own nurses and people whom you train at Madison, many of whom in the end go off for themselves."[15]

Young Dr. Julian Gant may have disappointed his Madison friends by practicing medicine in the Boston, Massachusetts area for 15 years. He had initially come to Madison as a student in 1922, taught there briefly, then later testified that Mrs. Scott made it possible for him to go to medical school. But he returned to Madison 20 years later in 1947 and served as chief of staff of the hospital for many years.

"Somewhere in the spirit of prophecy there is a statement, the exact wording of which I do not remember, but to this effect, that those who work in our institutions and who toil and slave and appear as a cart burdened down beneath sheaves will gain workers for the cause of God in the earth, but that on the other hand very many will repay them with naught but base ingratitude, apostasy and the like," Magan concluded. "More and more has this thought impressed itself upon me of late. Only a day or two ago I received a letter from one of our young men who has a very lucrative private practice, refusing to pay a pledge of $100 he had made to our new building because his father and the business manager did not get along well together. He admits he was wonderfully treated when he was in the school, that he was kindly helped in a thousand different ways, that he has all respect for the teachers and doctors who are sacrificing to carry on the work, but nevertheless he refuses to help us in order to take out his vengeance on the business manager. Well, I suppose it is only one way of gaining the blessing promised in the words

'Blessed are ye when men shall persecute you and revile you for my name sake.' A world of that will come to us from our own rather than from the heathen."¹⁶

Nevertheless, they were getting positive results.

"In spite of all of these things the work does go forward," Magan continued. "We have just had a call here from the Government of Bolivia to send them one of our young doctors. Mr. Henry Barron, who worked with Wellesley and Shaen for so long, is going provided they can wait long enough for him to get his little affairs shaped around so that he can go. The call is very urgent and Henry is anxious to get off if he can possibly get loose in the narrow margin of time allowed him. We have just recently had another wonderful providence in India where the Rajah of Bobbili has given us $50,000, equivalent in that country to about $250,000 of our money, with which to build another hospital. It is there that Sidney and Claire Brownsberger in all probabilities will go. Another one of our young men left this morning for Winnipeg, Canada, where he is starting medical missionary work with Elder Ruskjer."¹⁷

They just refused to surrender to the problems.

"And so the work goes and goes and goes in spite of everything," Magan stated. "I often think of it in the light of an experience I had once when I was crossing the Atlantic Ocean. We were in a terrible storm and one after another huge wave and a head wind were striking the vessel on the bow and causing her to shiver from stem to stern. It just seemed as if we were not making one particle of progress, and yet although we had that sort of a sea practically all the way from Queenstown to New York, and as I said, appeared to be making no progress whatsoever, we did get across. It is the same way with our work. I remember once when I was in Sister E. G. White's employ. She read to us at worship in her home one morning the account of Paul's shipwreck in the Book of Acts, and dwelt upon the verse which tells how they which could swim cast themselves into the sea, and the rest, some on boards and some on broken pieces of the ship, all escaped safely to land. I remember very well asking Sister White what lesson there was in that for us. She looked up with a kindly little smile, which was her wont, and said, 'Keep on splashing and you will get to shore.' I have thought of these words hundreds of times since. We all have to keep on splashing and we will get to shore."¹⁸

Percy Magan rose to great heights in the medical profession during these years, serving on important committees and being honored with important speaking engagements before distinguished audiences. The board of the College of Medical Evangelists elected him president of the entire institution in 1928.

By November of 1931, Dr. Magan was still very much involved in fund-raising and wrote to Dr. Sutherland about his work with other sources. He spoke of making contacts with people in the high places of the Southern Pacific Railroad and chances for returns. Then he referred to a letter from the brother of Lida Funk Scott and its ramifications.

"I do feel so thankful over Wilfred Funk's letter to Mrs. Scott. It cheers the soul in me," he wrote. "I have been thinking a great deal the last few days of those promises in that wonderful sixtieth chapter of Isaiah. Think of a few of them: — Verse 10, And the sons of strangers shall build up their walls and their kings shall minister unto them: for in my wrath I smote thee, but in my favor have I had mercy on thee.'"[19]

He seemed to be a living fulfillment of these words.

"This is a wonderful promise," he continued. "When we have done all that we can ourselves and our own resources are not sufficient the sons of strangers shall build up our walls. To me this spells Wilfred Funk, (younger half brother of Lida Funk Scott) Edward Harkness (a prominent philanthropist in the East with close ties to the Rockefellers) and people of that sort. And I love to talk to the Lord about them. They may not be godly Seventh-day Adventists, but I have a sort of an idea that they are just about as godly as Cyrus, Artaxerxes and others of their kind in days of old. As poor David Paulson used to say, 'Well, after all, God has an equity in some of these fellows outside of the truth.' That is certainly true, and he will use them to help us. The General Conference certainly did wonderfully by us and I am trying to impress it upon our folks that we must be loyal to them in our lives so that we will have a spirit and a heart to get under and carry forward the work, thus giving them a bit of good cheer."[20]

More promises from Isaiah 60 applied to their situation.

"Verse 11 : 'Therefore thy gates shall be open continually: they shall not be shut day nor night that men may bring unto thee the wealth of the Gentiles. ... Thou shalt also suck the milk of the Gentiles, and shalt suck the breast of kings: and thou shalt know that I the Lord am thy Saviour and thy Redeemer, the Mighty One of Jacob.' [verse 16]

"I gather it from this that God will so arrange things that we will not have to stop our work, 'thy gates shall be open continually.' He will provide means as we need it. And that money will come from the Gentiles. There will be a something about us that, to use the quaint Bible expression, will 'suck the milk of the Gentiles,' viz., a drawing power about us and the work we are doing that they can not withstand."[21]

Then Magan predicted what his Madison friends would get out of all their support of Loma Linda.

"But the best verse of all to me is the seventeenth," he wrote "'For brass I will bring gold, and for iron I will bring silver, and for wood brass, and for stones iron: I will also make thy officers peace, and thine exactors righteousness.' These words to me carry the thought that God is going to do far beyond what we expect of him. He will do abundantly above all that we ask or think. And again, if we are liberal with the little bit of brass that we may have as Madison has been so wonderfully liberal with the White Memorial, God will give you gold in return for it. Over and over again Mrs. Scott has come to our rescue here and often if she didn't have brass she has given us 'iron.' God will give Madison silver for that. He will give Madison brass for wood and iron for stones. You have always done so much for us here that I feel that the very least we can do is to stand by you in every way in your campaign with those folks outside of our faith. I am glad that we here at the White let the Loma Linda Division have $50,000 of White Memorial funds when they were so hard up, even although we could have used the money to good advantage ourselves. I am trying to get this spirit into our folks, that after all 'giving is getting.' And the more we will give up for the other fellow the more God will give to us from the sons of strangers."[22]

Asking his friends for money had given Percy Magan a new philosophy of life.

"Well, it is a wonderful work and a man that has learned the lesson that the mottoe [motto] should be not 'the world owes me a living' but owe the world a life' will get the farthest."[23]

The time came when Magan's Madison friends started coming to Southern California asking for money, and a special request showed the grip of the Great Depression on things there in the 1930s.

"Now, in regard to the matter of Mrs. Scott coming out here to solicit money for your building program, I want you all to understand that if Mrs. Scott does come I will do everything in my power to be of assistance to her," Magan wrote to Dr. Sutherland in 1931. "I have been a bit slow about writing you about this whole matter, but since I returned home from the East I have been in the tells over the matter of the Los Angeles County General Hospital. As you know, the Board of Supervisors of Los Angeles County is trying Dr. N. H. Hood for inefficient management and incompetency as an administrator. The idea is that some of them want to discharge him from his present position. The College of Medical Evangelists,-- I did not know it when I saw you, has been drawn into the fight on the ground that we are getting altogether too much out of the General Hospital. This certainly ought to stimulate us to do all we can to get our own Hospital up just as soon as possible. I was on the witness stand at the trial for about one hour and a half last Wednesday. It was up to me to prove that we were not getting special favors there and that we were paying for all we got. I think we made out a remarkably fine case, at least everybody tells us that we did. However, we must look for prejudice and hatred because of our religious principles and what the outcome of all of this will be I do not know.

"Now, while, as stated above, we will be happy beyond measure to do everything in our power for Mrs. Scott my own opinion is that it is almost useless her coming out here at the present time," he continued. "Every day here the depression grows worse and worse. We have thousands of dollars of pledges outstanding for our new Hospital building and collections on those are practically at a standstill. I greatly fear that Mrs. Scott would find very little favorable reaction toward her pleas from our doctor men as long as they find it impossible to pay pledges already made to their alma mater. I am sure you will appreciate how this is. Then when it comes to others,—take men like Mr. Nis Hansen. With all his land he is so desperately hard up now that he does not know which way to turn; sits up all night in a day coach when he goes to San Francisco so as to save sleeper fare. There is little or no sale, you may say, for anything in the line of ranch products in California, and bread lines are everywhere. Los Angeles County has been obliged to spend millions of dollars during the past year to feed and house the destitute. There was no provision in the budget for all of this money and the spending of it for these poor people has terribly crippled their enterprises.[24]

Magan still had fund-raising needs.

"We are trying to get in what little money we can for the David Paulson Hall which is to be our church building and general assembly hall," he stated. "It will possibly house the library also, but just how we are going to come on that I do not know. We must work it out for our other gifts to the building are dependent upon our getting these local donations."[25]

Times did indeed look grim.

"Now, this is the way things stand. Again let me say, that we want to do everything we can to help your work, but honestly, Ed, I don't think it would be one bit of good Mrs. Scott coming. You, with all your old friendships here might do something, but I doubt if even you could do anything worthwhile. This blowup in the Los Angeles County General Hospital I presume will make our Board feel that we must push everything in every way that we can for the new Hospital building. Whether we are going to have any success or not is a grave question. We would not, however, for this want to shut Mrs. Scott out, but we are just up against it. The outlook is certainly gloomy."²⁶

A letter written early in 1933 to Mrs. Scott reflected the hard times in Southern California, as well as the rest of the United States, were passing as well as her full recovery from depression after the death of her daughter.

"I can not tell you how glad I was to receive your most excellent letter of January 3 and I certainly appreciate your taking the pains to write me at such length, for I know you are a very busy person, always handling big matters which take a great deal of thought, planning and hard work," Dr. Magan wrote to Mrs. Scott.²⁷

He paid tribute to one of his departed friends in high places.

"I note what you say about Dr. Sanders' widow 'Miss Sara,'" he wrote. "1 have not had a line from her but hardly expected to. However, I would be glad to find out if she got my letters all right as I would not want in any way to have her think that I neglected her. Van Sanders was a very wonderful man, peculiar to be sure in some ways, nevertheless, with a heart as big as an ox in him. He was kindness itself to Dr. Sutherland and myself when we were in the University of Tennessee and Vanderbilt and I shall never forget his kindness as long as I live."²⁸

Dr. Magan was grateful to Mrs. Scott for giving him personal financial help.

"Your kindly words concerning our being able to get out into the country at last have cheered me a lot," he wrote. "I was afraid that some of you folks might think that during these hard times I was doing wrong to spend a penny to make any kind of a move. But, Sister Scott, the burdens here in the medical school instead of growing lighter have grown heavier and heavier as the days go by. We have more students and are carrying on more lines of activity than ever before. New things are coming up all the time, like the International Medical Foundation with its many ramifications which load me to the rails with work. It had come to me so that there was hardly an hour, figuratively speaking, of the day or night that either the doorbell or phone at our house was not ringing. For 17 years now I have been practically the only one of our teachers in responsible places who has lived on Boyle Heights anywhere near the Hospital. The result of this was that everything came to my door. The others dwell anywhere from eight to 10 to 15 miles away so that they were not easy of access. It was not only the visits and the calls themselves that took time and strength but the many things that hinged upon them and grew out of them.

"Now we have a nice little bungalow at 1738 Chelsea Road, San Marino, slightly over eight miles from here. This is on the property which you looked at and which by your kindly help I bought. Lillian is working hard and I endeavor to spend some time twice a week fixing up our lot, digging in the dirt, planting shrubs and the like. We are getting under way bit by bit, but of course we have only just moved in. It is very quiet out there. My telephone is 'long distance' as far as Los Angeles is concerned being a Pasadena number. This makes it better as we do not get the calls we otherwise would, and the ordinary run of people whom I should not properly let pester me find it much more difficult to get out there than they did to cross Bailey Street to New Jersey at the Hospital. So we are very grateful to you for all your kindness and little by little hope to make it a factor in keeping us going a while longer in this work. You have certainly been a wonderful friend."[29]

He had a different kind of financial concern this time.

"I am enclosing a copy in this of a letter I have written Dr. Sutherland," he continued. "I have just written Dr. Sutherland in regard to people who owe you. A while back I wrote him on the same matter and I think sent you a copy of that. I wish the letter could hold out more hopes of results than it does, but, Sister Scott, I am only writing Dr. Sutherland exactly as I believe the situation to be. The medical school has between $30,000 and $40,000 outstanding with students on money we have loaned them from the Student Loan Fund, and truthfully we are not able to get one penny of it. I have no doubt but that Tennessee is hard hit by the depression, but I doubt if it can be any harder, if as hard, hit as we are here. This country has profited tremendously by tourist trade. Now, speaking by and large, there are no tourists, there just isn't such a thing. There is very little sale for oranges, avocados and the like of our fancy crops from which so many people have been making their living. The big dairies here are pretty nearly all broke or about to break. Katherine Magan's father, Mr. Nis Hansen, who has been an old friend to Madison is on the rocks. At one time I suppose he was worth half a million dollars or more, but Wellesley and Katherine have been having to help them to exist.

"Now this situation affects our doctors. The boys are taking food, eggs, flour and the like by way of pay for their services. In fact, they are getting by any way that they can. Doctors here in the city both our own and those not of our faith are having a terribly hard time of it. It is related by men engaged in the real estate business and also by officials, I believe, of the Chamber of Commerce that 40 percent of the doctors in Los Angeles have defaulted on their rent. Men who have had immense practices like Drs. Thomason, Harris and H. M. Clarke and others are hardly able to squeeze along and how much longer they will be able to do it they do not know. I wish we could do more to help you to collect what is owing you, but I want to assure you, good lady, that we are working just as hard for you on these accounts you have given Joe and Nester as we are on our own.

"The County of Los Angeles has been feeding 148,000 people. By the thirty-first day of January the last penny of money which they have to expend for this purpose will be gone. They have already paid out to these poor folks $7.5 million. They have done this on a basis of giving 92 cents worth of food per week to each individual getting assistance in this manner. This has nothing to say to the help which has been rendered by the Community Chest and all the private and religious organizations like our own. The tuberculosis has increased in Los Angeles 27 percent since last April. When you think of six young women living in one room, only one of them having work and that at a very meager wage, and she trying to feed the other five as well as herself you can understand to what straits the people here are reduced."[30]

Some of the Madison boys were doing fine in medical school.

"You will be happy, I know, to learn that Joe Sutherland is doing splendidly," he wrote in concluding his letter. "So is Nester, and Cyrus Kendall is getting along all right."[31]

"My dear Dr. Magan," Lida Scott replied. "It was very fine of you to write me such a nice long letter and I very much enjoyed it. Your letters are always full of interest."[32]

What he did still satisfied her.

"I can well understand how the burdens that you carry at the Medical School make it necessary for you to get out and away from your work if you are going to last to carry these burdens as long as the Lord wants you to," she continued. "My work is heavy enough here, but I know your work must be so much greater than mine that there is no comparison, and you surely need to be where your mind, soul and body can receive refreshment and vigor for the duties that constantly present themselves.

"I hope someday to see your nice little bungalow at 1738 Chelsea Road, San Marino. I have seen the site, and can picture just about where you are. Is the orange grove still there and does it bear or has that all been ruined? I know that you enjoy fixing up your lot, digging in the dirt and beautifying the grounds generally. I am sure that Dr. Lillian must be enjoying it as much as you."[33]

Financially aiding the Madison medical school students remained a concern for her.

"I certainly appreciate, Dr. Magan, what you are doing for me in trying to get some funds for the medical graduates whom I have helped so that Joe and Nester and Cyrus can be helped. I am thankful if I can just get enough to help just Joe and Nester. I know the difficulty in the way. Everybody is having a hard time, and money is difficult to get hold of. It is very difficult for me and that is why I am so anxious to get a hold of it for the sake of those students. They are having a harder time than I like to see them have. The Medical School certainly has been generous with our boys and girls by loaning them money and often they do not try as hard as they might to get it back. Often they are selfish and thoughtless and often not honest."[34]

Mrs. Scott also felt the grip of the Great Depression.

"You speak of Tennessee being hit hard by the depression. I don't see how it could be much worse, and then, I suppose it could. The failure of the East Tennessee National Bank of Knoxville was a tragedy. Seventy thousand depositors went about wild. People cried in that old people lost every cent they had. I know of one aging woman who finds it very difficult to work, who has lost $600 which was every cent she had for her old age. Nearly everyone in Knoxville lost. They seemed to have absolute confidence in this bank. Some of them are taking the inevitable cheerfully and thoughtfully and are finding pleasure in helping others worse off. Such times often disclose nobility which we did not expect to find but others show a very different spirit.

"I am sorry that Brother Nis Hansen is on the rocks, after being so generous and kind to so many others. Mrs. Hurlbutt's farm at Clear Lake [northern Georgia] has gone on the rocks too. We inherited it at this time. The lovely Bartlet [Bartlett] pear orchard is doomed to ruin, also the nut trees are blighted. We did not get enough money off of the place to pay the taxes. So far it is a liability, though we hope for better returns some day, and it may be in such cold storage for a time of greater need."[35]

Mrs. Scott could find humor in hard times, however.

"Judge Wilkerson of Chattanooga asked me the other day if Madison was suffering from the depression," she wrote. "I told him, 'No, not more than always. We are used to it and know what to do.' He laughed."[36]

"My dear Sister Scott," Dr. Magan replied. "It was exceedingly good of you to go to so much pains to write me such a long letter and most deeply do I appreciate your thoughtfulness, as well as your many, many kindnesses to us here and to Lillian and me, personally. I know you have many heavy burdens to carry and if I know anything at all, the Lord has worked mighty miracles in Madison, Tennessee, and we have not seen the end yet. I cannot help but feel that as the days go by our general brethren, especially now that Elder Watson is president of our organization in Washington, will begin to see more and more in the noble work that has been carried on at Madison for so many years. Certainly the eternal God is vindicating the principles for which Madison has stood."[37]

He had good and bad news to report.

"We are having good days from one angle in the medical college at the present time. We are now organizing and sending out a group of nurses who are known as the Ellen White Nurses. These women are donating their time; the hospital is giving them their board; and the county is paying their car fare, etc., while they work among the very poorest and most starved classes in this city. This work is attracting a great deal of favorable attention. Our nurses in the school of nursing are spending a considerable amount of time giving Bible readings, health talks, and the like. This is a separate work, however, from that of the Ellen White Nurses. While patient attendance in hospitals throughout the country has dropped in the last year 40 percent we are only down about eight percent here at the White Memorial Hospital. We feel very thankful for this."[38]

His new home was working out well.

"Yes, we certainly do get wonderful peace and happiness in the little bungalow at 1738 Chelsea Road. The orange trees all died. There was no way, as long as no one was living on the place, to keep them fumigated and cared for and they were old trees anyway. However, now I have actually begun work on the lost and so has Lillian. We have planted a goodly number of young trees and I get my exercise with hoe on the lot. I do not get as much as I should, due to lack of time, but I am getting some for which

I feel very grateful. The house is a bit better than it should be but we were obliged to do this on account of the building restrictions in San Marino, and it was better to build on this lovely lot than to try and buy a place in some cheaper district elsewhere. Lillian spends a lot of time with her hoe, water pot, and wrist in the garden. We certainly feel very grateful to you for making all this possible for us.

"Wellesley and Shaen are having a hard time too. Their income is less than half of what it was awhile back, while at the same time they are doing more work than ever, but the poor people just don't have anything with which to pay. I believe, however, that this depression is doing our graduates a world of good in a spiritual way, and from that angle I am thankful for it.

"Val is at Pacific Union College. He is doing very well in very many ways. His health is far from good but he is working hard and trying to get along."[39]

Money was an ongoing problem.

"My dear Mrs. Scott, I only wish there was some way we could really accomplish something for you in the collection of funds for Joe and Nestor but we are simply not collecting anything, or next to nothing, on our own accounts. Mr. Hudson is doing just as much to try to collect your money as our own, but we simply cannot get it. There are some who could pay but I don't think we are going to get anything out of them unless we start suit, and it may have to come to this. One of the saddest things in this whole matter of helping students is the tremendous amount of ingratitude which we get. We have outstanding almost $40,000 of money we have loaned them; Dr. George Thomason has about $40,000 outstanding; Dr. Henry Westphal has about $20,000 outstanding; and none of us seem to get hardly a thank you, to say nothing of having our money returned. You were in the same place and I grieve for what you have suffered. Elder Watson was here the other day and counseled us to start suit for some who have simply annoyed us, and my advice to you, dear lady, would be to do exactly the same thing."[40]

Times were just hard.

"I am so sorry to read all you write about the depression in Tennessee and especially about the sad tale you have written relative to the bank at Knoxville. I had not heard about this. It is pitiful. The revelations in the papers the last few days concerning affairs in the gigantic banking institutions in New York have rocked California to its foundations. Confidence in anybody and everybody seems to be gone. The state of affairs in Michigan, where, as I understand it, every bank in the Lower Peninsula is closed, is appalling. Certainly these things spell the end of everything."[41]

Yet in spite of all the problems, Percy Magan was rising in the medical world of the West Coast.

"I am so sorry to know that your dear brother has had so much ill health, but glad that it has had a precious influence upon him. These things are many time blessings in disguise. Lillian is very frail. Just now I am busy fighting an anti-vivisection bill in the California Legislature at Sacramento. Recently, Governor Rolph was determined to put me on the State Board of Health and later on the State Board of Medical Examiners. I declined, but he wanted me to name a man for the State Board of Health, which I did, putting on one who has been an excellent friend of the school. I believe this is better than for us to go on ourselves."[42]

Dr. Magan continued operating on the highest levels of the medical profession during the Great Depression years and maintained a busy speaking schedule in addition to being head of the medical school. Health problems had always plagued him and began taking their toll as he grew older.

Lida Scott spent the 1930s at Madison promoting the off-campus work of Madison College, serving on the boards of its many "unit" affiliates in the South and carrying on extensive business correspondence with them through her office as secretary-treasurer of the Layman Foundation.

The final letters in this set were written during World War II, which brought another set of trials.

"You must be in turmoil in the Medical School with your doctors being called into the army and the students unsettled as to their future," Mrs. Scott wrote to Dr. Magan in August of 1942. "We are thrown into a dilemma from a letter which we received from the College of Medical Evangelists saying our students would not be accepted this year. Isn't this a rather late notice?"[43]

"No, we are not in any turmoil here in the Medical School," replied Dr. Magan, with this letter listing his title as President Emeritus of the College of Medical Evangelists. "We have things very well arranged with the Army and for that matter with the Navy. Every one of the men who wants to get into our school must be in the Army or the Navy Reserve, and then they let them alone until they are through their course. We made an agreement with the Army that we would let them have a certain number of teachers provided they would let the rest of our teachers alone, and we reserved enough teachers so that we could carry on our work; but, of course, things here on the Pacific Coast are unsettled. We, however, have more students by far than we had last year.

"This part of the country, however, is in a hard way," he wrote. "We are jammed with soldiers everywhere. At times the roads are packed with them—whole armies of military lorries, jeeps, peeps, and the like. Whether they are really expecting that this part of the coast will be raided or not I do not know, but the Army are certainly very active and so are the Navy."[44]

He then answered her question about the student admissions to the best of his ability.

"I have just read your paragraph stating that you are thrown into a dilemma through a letter which you received from the College of Medical Evangelists saying that your students would not be accepted this year," he continued. "I know but little about this but I think it lies in the fact that there was an action taken either by our Board of Trustees or Faculty, I am not sure which, that students wanting to enter the medical course must at least have had their third year premedical in an accredited school. Just how long a time the government will allow us to let this rule lie dormant before enforcing it I don't know, and it may be that we are pressing the matter too much in asking that it go into effect immediately, but we never know from hour to hour what the Army or the Navy will order."[45]

Madison College never became accredited.

Florence Fellemende, secretary of the Layman Foundation at Madison, wrote the final letter in the series on May 4, 1945.

"This is just to let you know that Mrs. Lida F. Scott, our Secretary-treasurer, died this morning at 5:05, after a two weeks illness. She suffered a heart attack two weeks ago today.

"Her funeral will be held here at Madison College, Wednesday, May 9, at 10 a.m."[46]

Percy Tilson Magan retired as president of the College of Medical Evangelists in June, 1942, and died on December 16, 1947, at the age of eighty.

Epilogue

On January 29, 1917, William C. White, believing that SDA periodicals were overemphasizing World War I as the fulfillment of Bible prophecy foretelling the end of time, wrote to A. G. Daniells that, with few exceptions, he found two categories of Bible and history teachers in Seventh- day Adventist schools. He described one group as being progressive and interesting but unorthodox. The other group was orthodox but unprogressive and boring.

Brother White urged the conducting of an annual summer school to develop some systematic method of improving Bible prophecy interpretation.[1]

The General Conference organized such a school lasting for six weeks, starting on July 1, 1919. It dealt with two conflicting views of understanding the visions of Ellen White. One school of thought saw nothing wrong with uncovering and correcting historical errors of fact. The other emphasized a "holistic approach" to avoid the need of deciding which historical statements were inspired or not.

While these delegates tried to agree on what to do about inspiration and revelation, E. A. Sutherland, Percy T. Magan, and Lida Scott were busy building the College of Medical Evangelists. In doing so, they became part of the "chosen few" Adventists of their generation.

They are thus tending to outshine some of their more prestigious contemporaries like John Harvey Kellogg and Arthur Grosvenor Daniells in Adventist history. Dr. Kellogg, who laid the foundation for Adventist medical work, was a man of unusual ability in many fields—medicine, education, business, writing, public relations—and became world famous through his high attainments. Arthur Daniells fulfilled an important historical principle of the church, namely, for an inspired religious movement to have staying power, the fervent revivals and acceptance of Bible truths must be followed through with organization. He developed a denomination capable of inspiring and preparing people to share the gospel anywhere in the world.

Both Dr. Kellogg and Elder Daniells were operating on the world stage when Sutherland and Magan were obscure college professors struggling and sacrificing to start new schools in Michigan and later in Tennessee as directed by Ellen White.

But while Dr. Kellogg disagreed with Ellen White by investing all his talent and energy into building a world-famous sanitarium in Battle Creek, Michigan, Drs. Sutherland and Magan followed the less-popular course of encouraging their graduates to establish smaller schools and sanitariums in many places of the South. While the Daniells administration stalled in upgrading the College of Medical Evangelists into Grade A status, Sutherland and Magan devoted themselves to developing it, taking Mrs. Scott with them into history.

Having less popularity and prestige to lose, they followed all of the Ellen White counsels. When she told them the will of the Lord, they did it without questioning whether or not it would be a good idea or the will of individuals wanting power.

The result was a denomination with a medical work of high standing in the world, an enduring monument to faith in action. The College of Medical Evangelists grew into Loma Linda University.

Within the Seventh-day Adventist Church, the medical professionals became elite members having little to do with preaching the gospel. The remarkable organization developed by Arthur G. Daniells commanded the respect of the Protestant world as being one of the best in Christendom, but "finishing the work" of the Seventh-day Adventist Church, or taking the "everlasting gospel to every nation, kindred, tongue and people," remained a vision.

Appendix

A letter of sympathy from Lida Scott to William C. White

22 Upper Mountain
AVE Montclair, N.J.
July 24, 1915

My Dear Brother White,

Mr. Scott called my attention to the notice of Sister White's death in the newspaper last Sabbath.

My heart aches for all of you, for it means so much to you in many ways, but it means much to us all, and I feel a sense of desolation akin to the feeling that the disciples must have had when the tangible evidence of the Lord's presence left them. His work was made unnecessarily difficult and trying because of the unbelief of the people who failed to appreciate the gift placed among us.

As for my part, I mean, by God's help, to erect in my life, by showing my appreciation of the counsel given to us, a monument that she would much appreciate, a life lived in harmony with the heaven sent principles. I wish we might all do this and how it would rejoice her heart upon the resurrection. We have reason to look forward to this glorious event with longing.

Please extend my sympathy to those who will feel the personal loss most keenly because of their past relations with her.

Give my love to your wife and children.

Most sincerely yours,

Lida F. Scott

P.S. Miss Coffin also sends heartfelt sympathy. L.S.

A fund raising attempt

At the 1915 Fall Council held at Loma Linda, California, a group of prominent Adventist women led by Mrs. S.N. Haskell agreed to lead a campaign to raise $61,000 to build a new teaching hospital in Los Angeles for the College of Medical Evangelists. Mrs. Haskell noted a large number of pioneer Adventist ministers at the meeting and persuaded seven of them over 80 years old to help by allowing a picture of them to be sold. These two photos on the following pages appeared with an appeal in the April 27, 1916, edition of *The Advent Review and Sabbath Herald*. "Because of the heavy burden carried by the servant of the Lord for this medical school, it seems fitting that the hospital should bear her name," Mrs. Haskell wrote in the accompanying article.

The ladies worked hard but did not bring in enough money to start construction of the Ellen G. White Memorial Hospital.

Left to right: S.N. Haskell, J.N. Loughborough, George I. Butler

Front row: S.N. Haskell, J.N. Loughborough, George I. Butler
Back Row: J.H. Rogers, J.O. Corliss, H.W. Decker, W.H. Cottrell

The Relation Between the School and the Medical Profession

(Abstract of a talk given at Madison, Tennessee, by Dr. E.M. Sanders, a prominent Nashville physician and medical school professor of Edward A. Sutherland and Percy T. Magan, and printed in the January 4, 1917, edition of *The Advent Review and Sabbath Herald*.)

I have been asked to say a few words in regard to the relationship between the works of this institution and the medical profession. I came here as a representative of the medical profession, and more or less as the mouthpiece of the people, because I hear what the medical profession and the people say about you when you are not present.

I congratulate you on the work you are doing. It is much more far-reaching than you realize. This institution stands for a high plane of moral living. I never knew any other people so imbued with high standards of life as are those who established this institution and have made it what it is today. They deserve great credit.

There is certainly a need for the kind of work you are doing, although it is hard work and has been hard all along. That is why you have found your place—because there was a need for it, and that need grows greater each day. More people live in the cities and country towns than formerly.

These small towns of yesterday are the busy little cities of today. They have their electric lights, late hours, coca-cola, stimulating drinks, heavy foods, overacting, 16-and-18-hour days. These conditions make necessary such places as this, where men and women can go for rest and receive treatments for mind, and body, and soul.

You have done a great deal, but what you have done is just a small beginning, though it is true it has been a wonderfully rapid work. There is a multiplying need for this work. We must depend upon you. I have talked to people who have met you only once. I have talked to people who have been here just one week. I have talked to people who have indirectly known of your work, and have not known you personally. And the influence of this work is beyond comprehension. The field has no limitations, and the possibilities for your work are beyond human conception.

The profession, the so-called regularly organized profession, has come to believe in this kind of institution, and you have even more friends among the laity than you have among the profession. But they will all come. The doctors will come— they have been coming.

It takes a long time to correct the false ideas of the people. An operation is a serious strain on the nervous system. It produces a shock and exhaustion, and it takes time to reproduce this waste, and to return to normal conditions. We are just fretting the profession to the place where they realize this. Without this understanding and harmony, we could accomplish but little. If we work against you, we work against ourselves: your work will not be so sought for, and our work will not be so beneficial. There must be harmony between the profession and your workers along these lines.

The country doctors must be brought into cooperation with you people who control these hill schools, and the doctors here should do their part in bringing this about. There are thousands of people in the country districts who are overworked, tired, and exhausted, who should be in these little institutions, where they can rest, where they will be away from the coffee pot, away from the strong pipe, from the Wine of Cardui and other patent medicines, a large percent of which is alcohol upon which they spend millions of dollars. These people need you. There is the broadest field of operation for these hill schools, with their treatment-rooms, their little sanitariums.

There is one idea I wish to emphasize, stick to your work! I am glad to know of the way your workers have gone out among these people, saying, "I am not a graduate nurse. I am not a doctor. I am just a worker." If you stick to that policy, your candor, your honesty, and your fixedness of purpose will carry you to a great victory in the end.

There is one very serious question that I want to mention, the most serious problem in your work, as I see it from my position on the other side of the fence, and that is your problem of obtaining a medical education. Your work cannot go on without doctors among your own people. You must have them. You cannot run this sanitarium without practicing physicians. You do not need them in your hill schools, but you must have more physicians among your people than you have now; and you cannot have them under the present conditions.

The time has come when you cannot graduate your boys and girls from our medical schools, because we run our schools on Saturday; and as you will not go to school on Saturday, you lose two days out of the week. You will either have to give up your religion, or build you a medical school. To get your school on a different foundation, you will have to raise money. That movement must start somewhere and sometime, and the sooner the better. You must get an endowment for your school in order to run it.

I could not come out here and say anything without acknowledging to your for myself, my friends, and to the people at large, our appreciation of the great work that the little band of men and women who founded this institution have done. There are a few great people in this country, and these men and women have a place among them. I know of their work, and I know more about what they have accomplished among our people than you know. I know the grateful patients. I know the loyal appreciation and gratitude we have for these men and women who have come to the south and established this institution, laying the foundation for one of the greatest works that is being done in our country.

A letter of appreciation to Lida Scott from the residents of newly-completed Montclair Cottage

304 N. Boyle AVE,
Los Angeles, California
January 5, 1918

Dear Mrs. Scott,

It is in appreciation of the beautiful and comfortable home in which we live that we write these few lines to you tonight.

The kindliness we feel toward you is not of an ordinary kind, for we realize that the spirit which moved our home into existence came from a self-sacrificing soul and a generous heart, and this knowledge makes the place dearer to our hearts and makes us admire you as a true woman who loves to minister to a needy world.

Also as we compare our dwelling places of last year with the present we are very very glad there was a Mrs. Scott who was interested in girls taking a medical training. About a year ago we lived in a place we called the "Ark." It was of such an ancient style with so much dirt accumulated in its corners you would think it had not been cleaned since Noah's time. But hope and cheer came into our hearts a few months later when Dr. Magan told us that Mrs. Scott's Building was going up next. And now our hopes are being realized.

The building is a neat and modern looking home with two stories containing 16 convenient and comfortable rooms extending half way around one side and one end of the building is a portico supported by five pillars and adorning the two entrances. The roof of the building is flat with a wall extending around it and can be used for an out-of-door sleeping place. The gas and solar heating system occupy a part of the roof space. Each floor has a neat and well- planned bathroom with bath tub and shower bath.

The rooms in which we spend many hours studying and sleeping have added much to our comfort and contentment of mind. Each room has what we call a "Jitney bed." It will roll anywhere you want it to in the room and can be shoved half way out of sight under the wall and used as a couch in the daytime. Above this porch is a built-in book case enclosed with glass doors which is very convenient. The closets are roomy with large drawers on one wall which in connection with the mirror on the closet door, we use as dressers. A table and two chairs is all the furniture needed for the room. The windows are French style which allow good ventilation, the screens being on the inside and roll up like window shades. This will give you some idea of the building but will not express the gratitude we have in our hearts to you, who made such a noble sacrifice that we might be contented and happy. The home you have erected for us will always be a bright spot in our memories and while we want to sincerely thank you it but faintly expresses our gratitude.

Maybe someday to meet you is our desire.

With warmest love,

Alma Larson
Esther Aalborg
Alice Beauchamp
Mr. and Mrs. Theron Johnston
Mr. and Mrs. E.R. Morlau
Harriett R. Bulpitt
M. Louise Guerne
Johannah Harel Daiv
Rosa B. Smith
Mary Borg
Bertha Wadsworth
Mary K. Anderson

Excerpt from a letter written by E.A. Sutherland to Dr. Lillian E. Magan, widow of Percy T. Magan, on September 22, 1952

"I do not know if you are aware of it, but Percy and I were together, closely associated, for over 30 years, forming a bond or tie that was very unusual and together we attacked a number of problems that were difficult and successfully worked them out. To illustrate, the moving of the Battle Creek College to Berrien Springs, and the establishment of Madison, both of which took a great deal out of not only ourselves, but out of you and Sally, [wife of E.A. Sutherland] I will not attempt to write you of the many tussles that Percy and I had with the brethren in the carrying forward of these most important movements. Everything has shown since that the providence of God was in our moving the college out of Battle Creek. It was the only Seventh-day Adventist Institution that did not suffer being burned out, then the location, the establishment of Emmanuel

Missionary College [now Andrews University] has proven to be also the result of God's guidance for it is one of our finest educational institutions.

"Then, the establishment and the conduct of Madison for over ten years under our joint direction has proved to be also a very important move, even though opposed bitterly by some of our leaders at the time. You can fully appreciate the satisfaction that we have to know that now the General Conference recognizes Madison as a unique and most important institution in carrying forward the self-supporting missionary work. They regard the plan as a pattern that they wish to see followed by the self-supporting institutions and groups conducted by the lay members of the church, so, God blessed the efforts that Percy, myself and others put forth in the founding of Madison.

"Then, too, when we were separated by the providence of God and Percy and you were called to unite with the College of Medical Evangelists we still pulled together, and I have heard Percy say a number of times that the union that existed between himself and myself was like that between David and Jonathan. When Percy was obliged to start the Los Angeles end of the College of Medical Evangelists, the General Conference was slow in putting up the funds. He had persuaded them to match dollars in the purchase of a site and the erection of necessary buildings. He put our long relationship of over thirty years to the acid test when he told me of the proposition that he had made with the General Conference and that he saw no way by which he could start his part of getting money without my being willing to allow money that had been promised Madison to go over to his project to enable him to get the General Conference to loosen up. Mrs. Gotzian who had been connected with Madison for sometime and had promised her funds to build up Madison was persuaded by Percy and myself to give to Percy the $10,000 necessary to purchase the block upon which the White Memorial Hospital and other buildings were built. Then next, in order to get money for the building we did the same thing with Mrs. Lida Scott. She had promised to put her money into the development of Madison, but Percy and I felt that the finest thing for Madison was to get the College of Medical Evangelists on its feet, especially the Los Angeles branch. So, I relinquished her from the promise she had made me, and she placed about $40,000 with Percy as a gift to enable him to have this duplicated by the General Conference.

"I mention these experiences that Percy and I had together because the friendship and relationship was so strong that we both felt that while we were separated, he in California and I remaining here, we were still partners and united in our efforts to carry on the self-supporting work. It was due to Percy's influence that Dr. Newton Evans and Dr. Thomason and yourself saw that Madison and the Southern field had every consideration given to it by the College of Medical Evangelists in the training of young people as physicians who entered the southern field. As a result, today the Southern Union Conference has more sanitariums than any other Union Conference in the world, and more selfsupporting institutions. All of this is due to the united efforts, to a large extent, of Percy, Mrs. Scott and myself in carrying forward this double program which I have mentioned. It is very clear that the Lord guided us from the time that we threw our interests together in Battle Creek to the time of Percy's death.

"You will pardon me for reminiscing, but I feel that a great deal has resulted from the cooperation of the College of Medical Evangelists and Madison.

Notes

References to the letters to and from Percy Magan, as well as the letters in chapter 2 from Downing and Evans, are from the Percy T. Magan Collection, Collection #229, found at the Center for Adventist Research, James White Library, Andrews University, Berrien Springs, Michigan.

Preface

1. In *The Later Elmshaven Years 1905–15*, volume 6, 428, Arthur White wrote, "On Friday morning, May 21, [1915] Mrs. Lida Scott from the East, came to the Elmshaven office to make acquaintance with W. C. White and to ask some questions about the church, its organization, and its stability. She was a relatively new convert, a woman of considerable means, the daughter of Isaac Funk of the Funk and Wagnalls Publishing Company in New York. She had spent some time at the Madison Sanitarium and School in Tennessee, self-supporting institutions. Now church leaders were currying her interest in the College of Medical Evangelists, and particularly in providing facilities in Los Angeles for clinical training of physicians." This book is on the Ellen G. White Estate web site at http://www.whiteestate.org.

Chapter 1: Setting the Stage—The Years 1910–1913

1. Quotes from this chapter are taken from the minutes of the Twenty-Third Meeting of the 1913 General Conference Session at Takoma Park, Maryland on May 29 at 10 a.m. A transcript of the proceedings is in the June 12, 1913, edition of *The Advent Review and Sabbath Herald,* vol. 90, no. 24, published at Takoma Park Station, Washington, D.C., 559–562.

Chapter 2: The Real Work Begins—The Year 1916

1. Letter, Augustus S. Downing to Newton Evans, MD, October 15, 1915.
2. Letter, Newton Evans, M.D. to Augustus Downing, October 21, 1915.

3. Letter, Augustus S. Downing to Newton Evans, M.D., November 3, 1915.
4. "The Los Angeles Hospital," *The Advent Review and Sabbath Herald*, December 16, 1915, vol. 912, no. 62, 8.
5. "Los Angeles Hospital," 9.
6. I.H. Evans, "The College of Medical Evangelists," *The Advent Review and Sabbath Herald*, vol. 39, no. 3, January 13, 1916, 6–7.
7. Letter, Percy Magan to Newton Evans, M.D., February 28, 1916. The letter itself reads:

   I have spent about a week with Mrs. Scott. The brethren in leading positions had given her to understand that the proposition which she made in regard to buying the home for the students in Los Angeles was all off, that Loma Linda could not accept an annuity of any kind. Consequently she made a deal with them and put this money into the General Conference on an annuity plan. However, I don't think we lost much, for really the terms are anything but favorable:—to wit— she let the General Conference have her Pennsylvania Railroad stock, amounting to about $40,000. They pay her five percent on it as long as she lives, and if she should need some of the principal or all of it at any time, she is to have it. I do not think it would have been a wise thing for us to have taken it on those terms, and those are the best terms she saw her way clear to give to them. "Therefore, I stuck to her for a straight gift of $5,000, and <u>got</u> it. She is to have it all paid to us before this year is out. Now you may think that this is not much, but it took lots of hard work to get it, and at the same time keep everything going sweet. The interest, which she receives off the Pennsylvania stock, is to be used by Mrs. Scott altogether for the education of youth in our schools and we are to have our share of this from time to time. I will get some of it for Gardner.

8. Mrs. S.N. Haskell, "Do We Need a Thoroughly Equipped Medical School?" *The Advent Review and Sabbath Herald*, February 24, 1916, 20. In this article, Mrs. Haskell quotes from *Gospel Workers* by Ellen G. White, 360. Also "The Door of the City Work," page 2 in the October 19, 1916, edition of the *Review*. The Ellen White quote in this article is from *Testimonies for the Church*, vol. IX, 167.
9. Percy T. Magan, "My Counsel Shall Stand, and I Will Do All My Pleasure," *The Advent Review and Sabbath Herald*, March 2, 1916, 16–17.

10. Percy T. Magan, "Strengthening the Hands of the Builders," *The Advent Review and Sabbath Herald*, March 16, 1916, 17–18.
11. Mrs. S.N. Haskell, "Medical Missionary Training College," *The Advent Review and Sabbath Herald,* April 13, 1916, 18–19.
12. S.N. Haskell, "Preparedness," *The Advent Review and Sabbath Herald*, May 25, 1916, 19–20.
13. W.T. Knox, "The Los Angeles Hospital," *The Advent Review and Sabbath Herald*, vol. 92, no. 20, April 20, 1916, 24.
14. I.H. Evans, "The Church Building for London," *The Advent Review and Sabbath Herald*, vol. 93, no. 31, June 22, 1916, 24.
15. Evans, "Church Building," 24.
16. G.A. Irwin, "What the Women are Doing at Loma Linda," *The Advent Review and Sabbath Herald*, June 1, 1916, 18.
17. Mrs. S.N. Haskell, "The Veterans' Aid to the Hospital Fund," *The Advent Review and Sabbath Herald*, vol. 92, no. 21, *The Advent Review and Sabbath Herald*, April 27, 1916, 20.
18. Mrs. S.N. Haskell, Cora B. McElhany, and Mrs. Lotta Alsberge, "What Our Women Have Done for the Ellen G. White Memorial Hospital," *The Advent Review and Sabbath Herald*, September 14, 1916, 2, 21.
19. I.H. Evans, "The Offering for Our Medical Hospital," *The Advent Review and Sabbath Herald*, September 7, 1916, 24.
20. "The Los Angeles Hospital," *The Advent Review and Sabbath Herald*, September 28, 1916, 2.
21. Letter, Percy Magan to Newton Evans, M.D. about Lida Scott:

    I have received the blue print for dispensary building and hospital [he wrote to Dr. Newton Evans on September 7, 1916]. I will write you in a day or two in regard to these. One thing worries me a good deal in regard to the hospital plans. I fear that if we build it upon the plans now suggested that the different units will be so close together that there will not be much light and air circulating between them. Our folks have made this mistake in regard to our new addition to the Sanitarium here at Madison. We have put on an addition on the east side, that is east of the kitchen and running parallel with the covering way which joins the parlor and side room units to the bath room units. This thing is so close to the other building that it looks like a dreary, dark, alley. Above all things let us avoid an effect of this kind.

    The more we can build on the cottage plan, the more unique, the more mission California style we can work into it the better. I have had a long talk with Mrs. Scott in regard to this. She is very strong in favor of the cottage plan. Of course I understand that she is not experienced in hospital construction and does not claim to know very much about it. But she is our friend and has given us much money and will do more and we must do all we can to satisfy the friends who are helping us liberally.

22. Newton Evans, M.D., "The Loma Linda Graduates— Where are They?" *The Advent Review and Sabbath Herald*, vol. 93, no. 42, August 24, 1916, 2.
23. Mrs. S.N. Haskell, "Report of the Women's Committee," *The Advent Review and Sabbath Herald*, vol. 93, no. 54, 2.
24. "Autumn Council of the North American Division Conference," *The Advent Review and Sabbath Herald*, vol. 92, no. 56, 7.
25. "Autumn Council," 5–6.

Chapter 3: Another Source of Money Emerges—The Year 1917

1. "The Ellen G. White Memorial Hospital," *The Advent Review and Sabbath Herald*, January 11, 1917, 15, 16.
2. Merlin L. Neff, *Invincible Irishman* (Mountain View, CA: Pacific Press Publishing Association, 1964), 100–112, gives a full account of the critical World War I years at the College of Medical Evangelists.
3. Letter, Percy Magan to Lida Scott, February 15, 1917.
4. Letter, Percy Magan to Lida Scott, August 21, 1917.
5. Letter, Percy Magan to Lida Scott, July 9, 1917.
6. In a lengthy letter written August 21, 1917, Dr. Magan wrote to Lida Scott about his miraculous visit with the Attorney General resolving the draft issue as well as other meetings with church and government officials.
7. Letter, Percy Magan to Lida Scott, August 21, 1917.
8. Letter, Percy Magan to Lida Scott, September 21, 1917.
9. Letter, Percy Magan to Lida Scott, August 21, 1917. Of the church officials at the Takoma Park meetings, F.M. Wilcox was editor of the Review & Herald, W. A. Spicer served as secretary of the General Conference. W.T. Knox was General Conference treasurer.
10. Letter, Percy Magan to Lida Scott, September 21, 1917.
11. Letter, Percy Magan to Lida Scott, September 21, 1917.

12. Letter, Percy Magan to Lida Scott, February 15, 1917.
13. Letter, Percy Magan to Lida Scott, February 15, 1917.
14. Letter, Percy Magan to Lida Scott, February 15, 1917.
15. Letter, Lida Scott to Percy Magan, July 16, 1917:

    Have received a fine long letter from Shaen, and all seems to be going well at Knoxville. After this course I suppose he will be moving on to Loma Linda. Can you let me know definitely what college expenses will be each year so that I can plan accordingly? In the present emergency I have been paying his railroad expenses and carfare which I will continue to do until he reaches Loma Linda. Then it was my proposition to pay only his tuition, board and books. Of course it will be necessary for me to pay for his board and room while at Loma Linda. While at Los Angeles is it your plan that he lives with you, and you furnish his room and board? How much then will be my part of the expenses? This information I should like to have and keep on file for future reference, as I must be sure that I make no larger promises than I can fulfill. I think we should be very clear so that we will each know what to expect. It has been, and will be a pleasure to educate Shaen medically, and I want you to feel that it is none the less so because I feel that the understanding on both sides should be definite. Shaen will then be able to make his plans, as he will know just what is to be expected of him. From past experience I believe we can count on him to do his part well.

    Shaen was one of three sons of Percy T. Magan. He married Ida May Bauer June 14, 1892. They had two sons: Wellesley Percy, born August 7, 1893, and Shaen Saurin, born September 24, 1896. His first wife died May 19, 1904. After moving to Madison in 1904, Magan married Dr. Lillian Eshleman August 23, 1905. They had one son, Val O'Connor, born January 19, 1912.

    Letter, Percy Magan to Lida Scott, July 9, 1917:

    I saw Brother Bowen and the Loma Linda treasurer, S.S. Merrill, relative to your matters. I showed Brother Bowen your letter in which you wrote me that you had already sent him an order to hand me $5,000 which I was to send to the Pacific Press. Brother Bowen could not find this order; neither could Brother Merrill. I then handed them the order for $13,000, and they have paid me this amount of money, but have not paid me the $5,000; so if you want to draw out $5,000 in addition to the $13,000 I think it would be well for you to either give me when I arrive at your place, or send them another note. I have made up to date the following disposition of the $13,000:

I re-indorsed to the College of Medical Evangelists one of the checks they gave, me in part payment of the $13,000 in the amount of $3,000 to cover the $3,000 which you wanted paid to make up the balance on your gift for the Helen Scott Cottage—White Memorial Hospital. This completes the original $5,000, and you have also sent me $1,000 extra, which I will refer to later. I am enclosing with this receipt from the College of Medical Evangelists for this $3,000.

Of the remaining $10,000 I have already sent $5,000 to the Pacific Press Publishing Association with the instruction to send you a note made out for one or two years, whichever suits them best (as I understood you to say that you were not particular as to the length of time for which the note should be drawn.) I have asked them to send this to you by registered mail so in case you leave Fletcher and it follows you over the country it will be safe.

I am writing Brother Quantock, cashier of the College View Bank, today, and asking him to place the remaining $5,000 on real estate mortgage at six percent if he can get that amount.

I am enclosing in this two receipts for you to sign. These Brother S.S. Merrill, the treasurer of the College of Medical Evangelists, has need for because of the fact that the promissory notes which cover the $13,000 which you paid him are locked up in the bank at Montclair, and you cannot return them to him for endorsement or cancellation. If you will kindly sign these and return them to S.S. Merrill, I will appreciate it.

I am also enclosing in this check of the College of Medical Evangelists #7174, on First National Bank of Redlands, in favor of Lida F. Scott, in the amount of $93.05, together with receipt for that amount, which Brother Merrill asks that you will sign and return to him. I understand that this is the payment of interest to June 30 on note dated April 23, 1916.

Now, if I have not made all of these matters clear I will endeavor to do so when we meet. It may be that if I do not get to see you on my way to Washington I may be able to stop there on my way back.

16. Letter, Percy Magan to Lida Scott, July 9, 1917:

Concerning the $1,000 which you sent me for the Helen Scott Cottage account, and which Dr. Lillian acknowledged while I was still in the East, I am this day sending Brother Bowen my check for $600 of the same, and will send him the balance as he needs it. I am handling it this way so that if there should be a little bit over from the building itself, I will have it for furnishings. If I turn it all over to him and there should be some over it would probably be thrown into the general hospital account.

July 6, 1917, letter from Lida Scott to Percy Magan:

I suppose you have been having great meetings at Loma Linda. We have remembered you and Dr. Sutherland and the Red Cross Summer School and the work which you are trying to accomplish every day in our prayers, and are eager to hear from you about your experiences.

I told Mr. Scott about the Helen Scott Cottage and showed him the plans. He seemed quite interested until he saw that it belonged to the White Memorial group. Then he objected strongly to my having Helen's name linked to that of a plagiarist, which Doctor Kellogg told him Mrs. White was. At first he commented that "Helen Gertrude Scott," and not "Helen Scott," ought to be put on the building if the name be inscribed there at all. They can call it the Helen Scott Cottage for short, of course, but her full name should be given. I am sorry this little incident in regard to Mrs. Ellen G. White's name should have stirred up all the old prejudice, but see nothing to do but to go quietly ahead and trust the Lord to help him to see the matter in a different light. I believe he will in time. Then on July 9, 1917, she wrote this letter: "I have been thinking it over about the Helen Scott Cottage and I have come to the conclusion that it would be better not to connect Helen's name with this cottage at all so long as Mr. Scott feels as he does about it. I told him I was going to write to you to do this, and it pleased him so much that I feel much better myself to have this change made. I told him that I would ask them at Madison to make the change in regard to the operating room if he so desired, but he seemed to feel that her name was all right there. We cannot blame him, for I know how I should feel to have her name connected with that of Mrs. Eddy or anyone else of whom I do not approve.

At the time of this correspondence, Lida Scott was recovering from personal tragedy. Her daughter, Helen Gertrude Scott, died July 28, 1914, at the age of 17. She later wrote in the March 24, 1920, edition of the Madison Survey that she went to Tennessee in August,

1914, "after I had experienced a great loss and was seeking for something of absorbing interest to soften and sweeten the sorrow."

Her husband, Robert Scott, never became a Seventh-day Adventist. According to the Madison Survey, he died April 15, 1946, at Madison Hospital, almost a year after the death of Lida Scott. His obituary said he was financial secretary of the Church of the Strangers in New York City as well as a teacher, author, and lecturer. He also was connected with Funk & Wagnalls for a number of years. The CME administration changed the name of the cottage to Montclair Cottage, which later housed medical offices on the White Memorial Hospital complex.

17. Letter, Percy Magan to Lida Scott, September 21, 1917.
18. Letter, Lida Scott to Percy Magan, August 5, 1917.
19. Letter, Lida Scott to Percy Magan, August 5, 1917.
20. "North American Division Recommendations," *The Advent Review and Sabbath Herald*, November 29, 1917, 7.
21. "My Sixty Years' Friendship with Dr. Magan," by Edward A. Sutherland, M.D., *The Journal*, Alumni Association, College of Medical Evangelists, March 1948, 30.

Chapter 4: Progress Despite World War I Threats—The Year 1918

1. Letter, Lida Scott to Percy Magan, January 25, 1918. This same letter shows her financial involvement with the College of Medical Evangelists. She later helped young Julius Schneider with more financial aid as well as took a serious interest on other young people according to her correspondence. On December 19, 1918, Dr. Magan wrote to her:

    Thank you so much for the check for $200 for Brother Julius Schneider. I received a statement from Brother Bowen covering his account the other day showing him indebted to the school approximately $133 and some cents. This covered the tuition for the first two trimesters and the balance, I judge, he was owing on board and room so I thought it best to apply the whole $200 on his account. This will pay up his tuition for the third quarter and leave, a balance of a few dollars on board and room. Just as soon as I get the receipt back from Brother Bowen I will send the same to you.

    Julius Schneider is a very worthy boy. He is peculiar, quiet, slow and stubborn as a Tennessee mule, but a good boy who never gives any trouble and he works very hard, and I believe is devoted to this cause. I have helped him some myself with money and clothes, but of course, my little store does not amount to very much in this kind of a game. Wellesley has had to have a good deal of help through this year as he only gets his board and $10 a month while he is interning at the Los Angeles County Hospital, and this has kept Lillian and I closer than we otherwise would have been. I do not know how we would ever have been able to keep Shaen in school if it had not been for all you have done for him. His clothes and incidentals, even though he is careful, have been quite an item.

After graduating from medical school, Julius Schneider worked for many years as an Adventist physician in the Atlanta, Georgia, area.

On October 20, 1918, Mrs. Scott wrote to Dr. Magan about three other young ladies:

Am glad that Miss Jensen is getting better. I have three girls who have come home from Madison with me. Miss Coffin is here getting her things together preparatory to returning to Madison; Miss Archie Meucke whom you probably remember, and Miss Lingham are planning to be with me throughout the winter. They are both convalescents. Miss Muecke is a fine girl and is anxious to have studies so that she can take an intelligent stand for the truth. Miss Lingham is a New England girl, a graduate of the Hemingway School of Domestic Science, a branch of the Framingham Normal School in Massachusetts. She is ambitious to devote her talents, training, and remarkable ability to the up building of community work among the mountaineers. She has spent a year at Smith, Kentucky. She is not an Adventist, but is one of the finest girls I have ever met and is open to truth. Both girls give a great deal of animation to our Bible studies. Mr. Scott is much interested in having them here. I am sure we shall have a most enjoyable winter together.

2. Letter, Lida Scott to Percy Magan, May 2, 1918.
3. "The Ellen G. White Memorial Hospital," *The Advent Review and Sabbath Herald*, May 2, 1918, 24.
4. Letter, Lida Scott to Percy Magan, May 2, 1918.
5. Letter, Percy Magan to Lida Scott, May 27, 1918.
6. Letter, Percy Magan to Lida Scott, May 27, 1918.
7. Letter, Percy Magan to Lida Scott, September 26, 1918.
8. Letter, Percy Magan to Lida Scott, July 18, 1918.
9. Letter, Percy Magan to Lida Scott, September 26, 1918.

10. "Loma Linda Institute of War Time Nursing," *The Advent Review and Sabbath Herald*, October 10, 1918, 16.
11. Letter, Percy Magan to Lida Scott, September 26, 1918.
12. Letter, Percy Magan to Lida Scott, July 18, 1918. Josephine Gotzian was an eledrly financial supporter of E.A. Sutherland and lived at Madison, Tennessee. May Covington inherited a prosperous farm in Minden, Nebraska. Percy Magan may have made friends with her family when he worked in that state as a new Adventist convert.
13. "Report of the North American Division Medical Department," *The Advent Review and Sabbath Herald*, May 9, 1918, 19.
14. Meade MacGuire, "Some Observations about taking a Medical Course," *The Advent Review and Sabbath Herald*, June 6, 1918, 14.
15. Letter, Percy Magan to Lida Scott, September 26, 1918.
16. Letter, Lida Scott to Percy Magan, October 20, 1918.
17. Neff, *Invincible Irishman*, 100–112, tells a full account of the critical World War I years at the College of Medical Evangelists.
18. Letter, Percy Magan to Lida Scott, December 19, 1918.
19. Letter, Percy Magan to Lida Scott, December 19, 1918.

Chapter 5: A New Era Opens—The Year 1919

1. Letter, Lida Scott to Percy Magan, January 17, 1919.
2. Letter. Lida Scott to Percy Magan, January 31, 1919.
3. Letter, Percy Magan to Lida Scott, February 13, 1919.
4. Letter, Percy Magan to Lida Scott, February 2, 1919.
5. Letter, Percy Magan to Lida Scott, February 13, 1919.
6. Letter, Percy Magan to Lida Scott, August 19, 1919.
7. Letter, Percy Magan to Lida Scott, August 19, 1919.
8. Letter, Percy Magan to Lida Scott, July 1, 1919.
9. Letter, Percy Magan to Lida Scott, August 19, 1919.
10. Letter, Percy Magan to Lida Scott, August 19, 1919.
11. Letter, Percy Magan to Lida Scott, August 19, 1919.
12. Letter, Lida Scott to Percy Magan, January 17, 1919.
13. Letter, Lida Scott to Percy Magan, January 17, 1919.
14. Letter, Lida Scott to Percy Magan, January 17, 1919.
15. Letter, Percy Magan to Lida Scott, February 2, 1919.
16. Letter, Lida Scott to Percy Magan, June 22, 1919.
17. Letter, Lida Scott to Percy Magan, June 22, 1919.

18. Letter, Percy Magan to Lida Scott, July 1, 1919.
19. Letter, Percy Magan to Lida Scott, August 15, 1919.
20. Letter, Percy Magan to Lida Scott, July 1, 1919.
21. Concerning Ellen White, Magan wrote:

    While her lifework and teaching were in harmony with truly scientific medicine, it was in the realm of the spiritual side of the healing art that she shone with a brilliance of holy luster. In the matter of appealing to men and women to regard their bodies as a sacred trust from the Highest One, and to obey the laws of nature and of nature's God, she stands without a peer. She it was who exalted the sacredness of the body and the necessity of bringing all the appetites and passions under the control of an enlightened conscience. Others emphasized science in health; to her it was left to impress the spiritual in the treatment of the temple of the body.

    No other one of modem day has entered this field of spiritual endeavor to anything like the extent she did. Her efforts were tireless from the days of her young womanhood to the hour of her death at a very advanced age. In books, in magazine articles, in papers, in tracts and pamphlets, she constantly and unswervingly called men and women, old and young, in clarion tones, to a more rational, a higher, purer plane of spiritual living. From the platform in churches and lecture halls, at convocations and conferences, her voice was continually heard urging the need of consecrated, Christian living in things relating to the body and its care. Others brought to light scientific facts concerning disease, its cause, and its cure; Ellen G. White drove home those facts on the spiritual side to the innermost citadel of the souls of men and women. (White, Ellen G., *Counsels on Health*, Mountain View, California: Pacific Press Publishing Association, 1951, 2–3)
22. Letter, Lida Scott to Percy Magan, August 4, 1919.
23. Letter, Percy Magan to Lida Scott, August 8, 1919.
24. Letter, Lida Scott to Percy Magan, August 17, 1919.
25. Letter, Lida Scott to Percy Magan, August 17, 1919.
26. Letter, Percy Magan to Lida Scott, August 19, 1919.

Chapter 6: The Final Showdown—The Year 1921

1. Letter, Percy Magan to Lida Scott, February 17, 1921.
2. Letter, Percy Magan to Lida Scott, October 20, 1921.

3. Letter, Percy Magan to Lida Scott, February 17, 1921.
4. These two ladies had helped Magan and Sutherland start Madison College in 1904. Nellie Druillard was business manager, Bessie DeGraw a teacher.
5. Letter, Percy Magan to Lida Scott, August 4, 1921.
6. Neff, *Invincible Irishman*, 117.
7. Letter, Percy Magan to Lida Scott, September 4, 1921.
8. Letter, E.A. Sutherland to Percy Magan, November 8, 1921.
9. *The Advent Review and Sabbath Herald*, June 8, 1905, 30.
10. Arthur G. Daniells, *The Advent Review and Sabbath Herald*, August 3, 1905, 6.
11. Letter, Percy Magan to Lida Scott, August 4, 1921. J.L. Shaw was an assistant secretary of the General Conference. M.E. Kem headed the youth work of the church.
12. Letter, Percy Magan to Lida Scott, August 4, 1921.
13. Letter, Percy Magan to Lida Scott, November 10, 1921.
14. Letter, Percy Magan to Lida Scott, November 10, 1921.
15. Letter, Percy Magan to Lida Scott, October 18, 1921.
16. Letter, Percy Magan to Lida Scott, October 18, 1921.
17. Letter, Percy Magan to Lida Scott, October 24, 1921.
18. Letter, Percy Magan to Lida Scott, September 4, 1921.
19. Letter, Percy Magan to Lida Scott, August 4, 1921.
20. Letter, Percy Magan to Lida Scott, May 20, 1921.
21. Letter, Percy Magan to Lida Scott, May 20, 1921.
22. Letter, Percy Magan to Lida Scott, August 4, 1921.
23. Letter, Percy Magan to Lida Scott, September 4, 1921.
24. Letter, Percy Magan to Lida Scott, May 20, 1921.
25. Letter, Percy Magan to Lida Scott, August 4, 1921.
26. Letter, Percy Magan to Lida Scott, October 20, 1921.
27. Letter, Percy Magan to Lida Scott, October 20, 1921.
28. Letter, Percy Magan to Lida Scott, August 4, 1921.
29. Letter, Percy Magan to Lida Scott, September 4, 1921.
30. Letter, Percy Magan to Lida Scott, October 18, 1921.
31. Letter, Percy Magan to Lida Scott, October 31, 1921.
32. Letter, Percy Magan to Lida Scott, September 14, 1921.
33. Letter, Percy Magan to Lida Scott, August 4, 1921.
34. Letter, Percy Magan to Lida Scott, August 4, 1921.
35. Letter, Percy Magan to Lida Scott, October 24, 1921.
36. Letter, Percy Magan to Lida Scott, October 24, 1921.

37. Letter, Percy Magan to Lida Scott, October 31, 1921.
38. Letter, Percy Magan to Lida Scott, October 31, 1921.
39. Letter, Percy Magan to Lida Scott, November 25, 1921.
40. Letter, Percy Magan to Lida Scott, November 25, 1921.
41. Letter, Percy Magan to Lida Scott, November 10, 1921.
42. Letter, Percy Magan to Lida Scott, November 10, 1921.

Chapter 7: Loma Linda Marches On—Post-1921 Letters

1. *The General Conference Bulletin*, Mountain View, California, May 24, 1022, vol. 9, no. 10, 228; May 25, 1922, vol. 9, no. 11, 249.
2. Neff, *Invincible Irishman*, 120.
3. Letter, John Harvey Kellogg to Percy Magan, December 5, 1922.
4. Letter, John Harvey Kellogg to Percy Magan, December 5, 1922.
5. Letter, Percy Magan to Lida Scott, January 19, 1923.
6. Letter, Percy Magan to Lida Scott, January 19, 1923.
7. Letter, Percy Magan to Lida Scott, January 19, 1923.
8. Letter, Percy Magan to Lida Scott, January 19, 1923.
9. Letter, Lida Scott to Percy Magan, April 23, 1923.
10. Letter Percy Magan to E.A. Sutherland and Lida Scott, January 13, 1926.
11. Letter Percy Magan to E.A. Sutherland and Lida Scott, January 13, 1926.
12. Letter, Percy Magan to Lida Scott, June 2, 1926.
13. Agreement between Percy Magan and The Layman Foundation, February 21, 1929.
14. Letter, Percy Magan to Lida Scott, March 3, 1929.
15. Letter, Percy Magan to Lida Scott, March 3, 1929.
16. Letter, Percy Magan to Lida Scott, March 3, 1929.
17. Letter, Percy Magan to Lida Scott, March 3, 1929.
18. Letter, Percy Magan to E.A. Sutherland, November 1, 1929.
19. Letter, Percy Magan to E.A. Sutherland, November 1, 1929.
20. Letter, Percy Magan to E.A. Sutherland, November 1, 1929.
21. Letter, Percy Magan to E.A. Sutherland, November 1, 1929.
22. Letter, Percy Magan to E.A. Sutherland, November 1, 1929.
23. Letter, Percy Magan to E.A. Sutherland, May 27, 1931.
24. Letter, Percy Magan to E.A. Sutherland, May 27, 1931.
25. Letter, Percy Magan to E.A. Sutherland, May 27, 1931.

26. Letter, Percy Magan to Lida Scott, January 26, 1933.
27. Letter, Percy Magan to Lida Scott, January 26, 1933.
28. Letter, Percy Magan to Lida Scott, January 26, 1933.
29. Letter, Percy Magan to Lida Scott, January 26, 1933.
30. Letter, Percy Magan to Lida Scott, January 26, 1933.
31. Letter, Lida Scott to Percy Magan, February 28, 1933.
32. Letter, Lida Scott to Percy Magan, February 28, 1933.
33. Letter, Lida Scott to Percy Magan, February 28, 1933.
34. Letter, Lida Scott to Percy Magan, February 28, 1933. The Huributt Farm later became Georgia Cumberland Academy near Calhoun, Georgia.
35. Letter, Lida Scott to Percy Magan, February 28, 1933.
36. Letter, Percy Magan to Lida Scott, February 29, 1933.
37. Letter, Percy Magan to Lida Scott, February 29, 1933.
38. Letter, Percy Magan to Lida Scott, February 29, 1933.
39. Letter, Percy Magan to Lida Scott, February 29, 1933.
40. Letter, Percy Magan to Lida Scott, February 29, 1933.
41. Letter, Percy Magan to Lida Scott, February 29, 1933.
42. Letter, Lida Scott to Percy Magan, August 17, 1942.
43. Letter, Percy Magan to Lida Scott, August 24, 1942.
44. Letter, Percy Magan to Lida Scott, August 24, 1942.
45. Letter, Florence Fellemende to College of Medical Evangelists, May 4, 1945.

Epilogue

1. Haloviak, Bert. "In the Shadow of the 'Daily:' Background and Aftermath of the 1919 Bible and History Teachers Conference. A paper presented at the meeting of Seventh-day Adventist biblical scholars in New York City on November 14, 1979." He quoted from a letter W.C. White wrote to A.G. Daniells on January 29, 1917. It is on file in the WCW Correspondence Book No. 116 for 1917–19—D-E at the Ellen G. White Estate, Silver Spring, Maryland. This complete paper is on the General Conference Department of Archives web site at adventistarchives.org. Click on Archives and Statistics Research Papers.

TEACH Services, Inc.
PUBLISHING

We invite you to view the complete
selection of titles we publish at:
www.TEACHServices.com

We encourage you to write us
with your thoughts about this,
or any other book we publish at:
info@TEACHServices.com

TEACH Services' titles may be purchased in
bulk quantities for educational, fund-raising,
business, or promotional use.
bulksales@TEACHServices.com

Finally, if you are interested in seeing
your own book in print, please contact us at:
publishing@TEACHServices.com

We are happy to review your manuscript at no charge.

www.ingramcontent.com/pod-product-compliance
Lightning Source LLC
Chambersburg PA
CBHW070542170426
43200CB00011B/2523